Digital Television Strategies

Business Challenges and Opportunities

Digital Television

Strategies

Business Challenges and Opportunities

Alan Griffiths

palgrave
macmillan

© Alan Griffiths 2003

First published 2003 by
PALGRAVE MACMILLAN
Houndmills, Basingstoke, Hampshire RG21 6XS and
175 Fifth Avenue, New York, N.Y. 10010
Companies and representatives throughout the world

PALGRAVE MACMILLAN is the new global academic imprint of the Palgrave
Macmillan division of the St. Martin's Press LLC and of Palgrave Macmillan Ltd.
Macmillan® is a registered trademark in the United States, United Kingdom and other
countries. Palgrave is a registered trademark in the European Union and other
countries.

ISBN 0–333–99295–4 hardback

This book is printed on paper suitable for recycling and made from fully
managed and sustained forest sources.

A catalogue record for this book is available from the British Library.

Editing and origination by Curran Publishing Services, Norwich

10 9 8 7 6 5 4 3 2 1
12 11 10 09 08 07 06 05 04 03

Printed and bound in Great Britain by
Creative Print & Design (Ebbw Vale), Wales

For Marjorie Griffiths, my first teacher

Contents

List of figures

List of tables

Acknowledgements

This book would not have been possible without the support and influence of many people. First and foremost is my wife, Gill, whose common and business sense have always made it possible for me to undertake the most testing challenges; such as writing a book while starting up a new business.

One of the great delights of a book about digital television is that it cannot be written in a library as there is almost no literature on the subject. Digital television is too new to have been classified. Consequently all supporting evidence for my arguments has come from newspapers and, most importantly, interviews recorded with important thinkers in the field of digital television. A list of all who have given the interviews in this book follows.

Many people have helped with the quick thinking and the sheer logistics required by a book like this. Kevin Green, one of the most devoted readers I know, advised strongly against the original idea of running transcripts at length. As a result extracts from interviews are incorporated as quotes in the argument. I believe this gives the book a pace it would otherwise have lacked. I am indebted to the patience of Stephen Rutt, Publishing Director of Palgrave Macmillan, who managed to keep this book to a publishing schedule which preserves its topicality. I am also grateful to Belinda Harley for backing him up – and promoting my literary career.

Many people have helped with the logistics. Peter Wright, Vice President of MTV Broadcast Services, was invaluable in helping to get the excellent session with Simon Guild. Gilly Cookson worked tireless co-ordinating interviews with NDS's top thinkers on set top box design. Robert showed me the power of games machines and their implications for the future of digital in the home. Anna distracted me with questions about the English Civil War, which I enjoyed. Graham Howes accommodated me in Cambridge, and worked hard at getting me into the University Library where I was able to ascertain that there are no books on digital television – except now for this one.

And finally Rebecca Marmot kept smiling at my clients for me when I was deep in thought about digital television.

Kingston Gate   Alan Griffiths

Interviewees

The author gratefully acknowledges the co-operation and time given by the following leading thinkers on digital television. They have all grappled with the complexities and implications of the most important change to happen to television since its inception, and shared their conclusions with me for this book.

Interviewee	Role
Paul Robinson	Senior Vice President, Walt Disney Television International
Greg Dyke	Director General, BBC
Peter Bazalgette	Chairman, Endemol UK
Rupert Howell	Managing Director, Chime Communications plc and founder HHCL
Rahul Chakkara	Director of Interactive Television, NDS
Rupert Miles	CEO Reuters Kalends and former Director of Interactive Television, Carlton TV
Eric Salama	Director, WPP plc
Dr Jas Saini	Vice President, Consumer Devices, NDS
Dr Graham Wallace	Director of Network Development, Kingston Communications plc
Richard Brooke	Former Finance Director, BSkyB. Director St James' Ventures
Simon Guild	Chief Operating Officer, MTV Networks Europe
Matthew Symonds	Associate Editor, *The Economist*
Sid McGrath	Planning Director, HHCL
Terry Marsh	Former Controller of Programmes, the Sci Fi Channel, and digital television consultant
David Whittaker	Business Development Manager, NDS

Re-Inventing Television

For over forty years there was little significant technological change to television. The biggest technical transition was the introduction of colour. But viewers could do little to determine what they watched, or how it was scheduled.

In the late 1990s some media groups decided to take advantage of a new technology to beam television into the home. This technology involves turning television signals into computer code. While this might sound like a matter which would only interest adenoidal engineers, it has profound implications for television: both for how it is viewed and how it works as a business. It changes the nature of television. It allows the viewer to apply the power and influence which they have in the world of retailing to the television market. Most of the television industry has been taken by surprise by this development – particularly as the audience they had been serving for the last four decades seems suddenly to have changed the habits of a lifetime. They have become an audience that makes unreasonable demands, wants exactly what it wants now, and uses the technology in ways that its inventors had not predicted at all.

The most disturbing implication for broadcasters is that television is now intimately linked with the fastest changing technology on earth – that of the computer. For years, Silicon Valley has been used to businesses (and business models) linked to computers which come and go in twelve months flat. They are not sentimental about this. That is simply the nature of information technology.

Digital television, like a carousel released from the top of big dipper, has embarked on just such a bumpy journey. In truth, no one really knew in 1997 which forms of digital television would work and which would fail. As a result there have been some spectacular mistakes – and some investors have lost a lot of money.

It is Europe which has climbed this learning curve fastest. This is because the take up of digital TV has been steepest there – with 39 per cent of households in the UK and France now with digital, compared with only 32 per cent in the US. What has happened in

Europe – the triumphs and disasters – will soon be visited on the US too. Digital television is like nothing which has gone before – and it cannot be treated as 'business as usual', as American broadcasters are about to discover.

Digital television is already having an impact on viewing, and on how television works as a business – and so on investment strategies in media. Its implications for advertising are so serious that this theme is considered in depth in this book. Advertising is not simply going to suffer a change in spending patterns but also a major structural change, due to the impact of digital television and the way it changes the behaviour of the television viewer.

Digital television's implications also reach wider. It will accelerate social trends which are present now in how people live and think. It also has implications for politics and the political process.

This book analyses who the winners and losers will be in the reinvention of television. It examines the strategies of the present players, and shows what works in their businesses and what is doomed to disappoint.

This is a business book. Many business books give the impression that once a strategy is determined its execution follows as cleanly as a robot building a car.

But in reality business is not like that. It is more like war – strategies help, but the presence of a decision maker is crucial in the fog of battle. As digital television is in its infancy, and because the fog and noise of battle is overwhelming, this book has tried to reflect that environment. It has done this by interviewing many of the leading players and incorporating their comments – for illustration or to provide colour – into the argument. The author believes that this gives a more accurate and vivid sense of the atmosphere in which critical business decisions are taken.

The critical decisions in the future development of the most powerful medium on earth are being taken right now. That is what this book is about.

What Is Digital Television, and Why Does It Matter?

TECHNOLOGY, COMMUNICATION AND CHANGE

Communication of any kind has always been transformed by technological change. And technological change in communication has always produced profound social changes. The creation of the printing press allowed the mass printing of the Bible. Liberated from the hands of omnipotent priests, all kinds of strange revolutions began to occur – starting with the growth of Protestantism and then leading to radical nonconformism, revolutionary publications and the overthrow of kings.

So when in 1894 a local farmer with a gun disappeared over a hill out of sight of the Marconi household to signal whether young Gugliemo really could send signals through the air to a distant electronic receiver, the resounding retort that rang out over the Tuscan hillside heralded more than just a local oddity.

The die was cast when the British military managed to use Marconi's equipment to send signals over nine miles across Salisbury plain. Marconi recalled that 'the calm of my life ended there'.

The ability to communicate electronically over large distances started a series of technological developments that culminated in simultaneous mass viewings of electronic content – unprecedented, in fact, in the history of publishing. While the Bible had been printed for mass distribution, the largest number of people who had ever received it before simultaneously had been restricted to the capacity of a church.

Television changed that. In the latter half of the last century it was possible to reach mass audiences which were watching the same programme simultaneously using electronic transmission. The effect on the viewers' psychology and on their buying habits was immediate and devastating, and was quickly noticed by product owners:

. . . when *The $64,000 Question* opened the results were sensational . . . ratings began high and climbed higher. On each program actress Wendy Barrie did stylish commercials for a new Revlon product, *Living Lipstick*, but in September the *Living Lipstick* message was suddenly omitted. A commercial for *Touch and Glow Liquid Makeup Foundation* was substituted because, it was explained, *Living Lipstick* was sold out everywhere. Stores were phoning the factories with desperate pleas for additional shipments. Hal March, master of ceremonies, pleaded with the public to be patient. The program was drawing an 84.8 per cent share of the US audience.

(Erik Barnouw)

So by 1952, when *The $64,000 Question* hit the airwaves, television's strange power to create mass audiences was gaining the shocked attention of companies and governments.

Analogue, scarcity and monopoly

The television technology which produced this phenomenon was analogue broadcasting – it is what Marconi invented. It was his legacy, and it survived unchallenged for almost exactly 100 years. It had one important hidden characteristic which didn't become truly apparent until the birth of digital technology at the end of the century: scarcity. Analogue broadcasting, through its very nature, made space on the airwaves scarce.

The reason for this is that analogue signals are unencoded. They involve 'flexing' the medium which carries them in exactly the same way in which the signal that they are carrying itself 'flexes'. It is rather like speaking underwater. The water pulsates to the same rhythm as the voice – and so is heard by anyone immersed in the water. Because twentieth century television signals were exactly analogous to what was being transmitted they could be intercepted anywhere with a rudimentary receiver and viewed. And that is what happened. Analogue television was free to air for all of its first forty years, as it was impossible to prevent people watching it except by removing their televisions. The idea of 'conditional access' and 'pay per view' was then a distant dream.

Analogue produced scarcity because flexing the spectrum in rhythm with an entire television picture gobbled mammoth chunks of electromagnetic spectrum. The mathematics of it meant that most countries could only support five analogue channels trans-mitted through masts – and the fifth one badly.

It was this scarcity which produced television's tremendous early power. With only five channels (and typically with the fourth and fifth a miracle of spectrum juggling) television channels easily became monopolies – and acted monopolistically.

In America this resulted in 'state sanctioned monopolies'[1] as Michael Powell, Chairman of the Federal Communications Commission, has called them. It also led to the type of business model which traditional broadcasters find natural to this day. It can be represented by a simple supply chain (Figure 1.1), in which the most important and powerful parts are the channels.

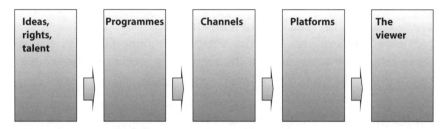

Figure 1.1. The parts of the basic television supply chain

In the 'monopoly' television model, although programmes cannot be made without ideas, rights and talent they are commissioned by mighty controllers of channels. Channels are the only paths to the viewers because, being provided by a monopoly, they are the only way in which viewers can receive television content. The 'platform' is the technical means by which the viewer gains access to programmes. For forty years it was completely standardised as analogue television transmission. Television could only be received through one device – an analogue television receiver. This had the curious effect of making traditional broadcasters believe that this last vital link to the viewer, the reception platform, was insignifi-cant. Television had always been received like that so it would continue to be received like that. And spectrum would be scarce. And advertising rates would remain sky high, as television was such a powerful and scarce medium that it could charge top dollar for its airtime.

This meant that the *channel* part of the chain was the most powerful and where the highest profit margins could be found.

Advertising poured into channels. Channels redistributed advertising dollars to other parts of the chain. This led to a business model which was an oddity – a publishing medium which was *entirely* supported by advertising revenue. No publishing medium before (or since) has managed this. Newspapers, for example, rely on a number of revenue streams such as cover price, advertising and sponsored 'advertorials'. But commercial television could survive, despite the enormous costs of programme production and staff salaries, on advertising revenue alone.

In the UK, France and Germany, public service television monopolies were also established which leaned heavily on the power of TV to charge high advertising rates. The exception was the BBC in Britain. As it was supported by a television tax and refused advertising, it led to artificially and grossly inflated advertising rates on its rival commercial channels.

The cosy assumptions of the television monopolists were shattered by two swift changes in the technology which television uses to get programmes to the viewer.

Multichannel

The first crack in monopoly broadcasting, which appeared in the early eighties, was multichannel. This took two forms:

- Satellite broadcasting
- Cable broadcasting.

Although these were both analogue technologies, they undermined terrestrial broadcasters' control of the platform to the viewer. For the cost of a box and a subscription viewers could hook up to about thirty channels containing programmes in a profusion which was unavailable on 'through the air' electronic broadcasting.

In the States cable take-up was driven partly by content, and also by the fact that in many areas electromagnetic transmission had led to poor reception. Some viewers thought that TV pictures always had a snowstorm across them until they encountered cable reception.

In Europe take-up was mainly driven by a single important factor: football rights. This was one of the terrestrial broadcasters' weakest spots. The very spectrum scarcity which had made them rich had also long deprived viewers of football games the chance to see their team play – a subject about which they were passionate. It was a lesson the terrestrial broadcasters never forgot, and which led them over-value football rights. European terrestrial broadcasters seriously began to believe that the only thing mass audiences cared about was football. In the UK the main commercial channel, ITV, cleared out its main family Saturday schedule to make way for football. It had to justify the amount it had paid for the rights. The experiment flopped badly, as ITV chiefs remembered that football appealed to only about a third of the audience.

It was US entrepreneurs, however, who understood quickly the true significance of multi-channel technology – its ability to create new networks. Because of the size and spending power of the US market a network was a valuable thing simply because of the vast potential size of its audience. Atlanta entrepreneur Ted Turner also realised that former 'minority interest' content, such as news, would be viable if it could be networked. So he collected enough cable franchise carriage rights in the States to produce 'Cable News Network' – the three most important components of the business model being listed in its title. Few people now recall what CNN stands for – but its clever exploitation of cable technology to collect an upmarket and commercially attractive audience was a world first.

CNN and a cable-networked pop channel, MTV, then moved to the next logical step. If it was possible to use multichannel to create an American network, why not create a *global* network? This was an expensive exercise, and often meant American broadcasters running up against baffling European regulatory regimes for the first time. One entrepreneur managed to negotiate carriage rights on all the cable systems in all the German Länder. This was so difficult to achieve that when the channel which it carried went bust the cable rights alone paid off all its debts.

However, global networks were eventually established using multi channel analogue. Sumner Redstone, the President of Viacom, is fond of reminding audiences that MTV reaches '340 million homes in 140 countries in 17 languages . . . a breathtaking total reach of one billion people making it by far the world's largest television operation'.[2]

Multichannel also brought a shock to the television environment – it shifted where good margins and revenues could be found to rights and talent owners (like the football clubs). It is very unusual to have a value chain where the greatest profits are located in the first stage of that chain. It normally signifies that all the subsequent links are adding little or no added value. And, indeed, in the multichannel revolution it is possible to see arguments which support this analysis:

- Little distinction between channels – so that some channels are perceived to be simply a 'means of receiving programming' and to have no identity of their own.
- A lot of very similar programming – really because programme making had been done for a restricted number of terrestrial channels, and there was not enough variety between programme types to support multichannel.
- Audiences' disillusion with the multichannel proposition (particularly in Europe). The criticism that there were 'thirty channels and nothing on' was very common in the eighties. It was reflected in high rates of 'churn' – the percentage of people who subscribed to a multichannel service and then cancelled within a year. For cable and satellite in the eighties this was running at about 22 per cent.

Multichannel also gave rise to the creation of something new – the television platform. In digital this becomes absolutely critical to television consumption, but in multichannel it was merely a way of ensuring that the viewer had access to the channels, delivered either by cable or satellite, to which they had subscribed. At the very heart of the multichannel box was the software that allowed such access: the 'conditional access system'. Rupert Murdoch was one of the first entrepreneurs to see the significance and importance of this software. He found a company in Jerusalem in Israel which could produce an unbreakable conditional access system,[3] and used it in the first generation of Sky boxes. Murdoch then realised that this software was of such strategic importance to his television operations that he bought the company that made it, NDS, in which News Corp still owns 80 per cent of the equity.

The leap into digital

The first digital television operation to launch in the world was Canalsatellite[4] of France, followed by TPS (also of France) and then by SkyDigital (Murdoch's UK based operation) in October 1998.

It is remarkable that all these operations went for digital technology so quickly as at the time all were still losing significant amounts of money on their multichannel operations. Essentially the decision to switch to digital owed much to the faith and vision of the boards of these companies, but there were also benefits from a business point of view:

- Far more bandwidth – so many more channels could be transmitted. Importantly, it also meant that there was enough bandwidth to allow viewers to start a movie at fifteen-minute intervals (this is called 'near video on demand').
- Far more sophisticated tracking of viewer habits and purchases.
- True video on demand – the ability for the viewer to see short clips of video exactly when they want them.
- The ability to provide interactive entertainment (such as games and betting).
- Far more sophisticated ways of guiding the viewer to what was on the service – through devices like the electronic programme guide – and personalisation.
- It allows pay-per-view for events and movies, as the digital conditional access system is far more sophisticated than its analogue multichannel equivalent. This is a very important element in increasing the revenues raised from each digital customer.
- Very importantly – the ability to upgrade the software in the box through a download from the satellite. This allows constant refreshment of the features and functions of the box, and means that the technology inside it can respond to changes in the digital television market. It also gives a digital platform the chance to enhance its competitive advantage over other television services.

All these features, and their implications for what digital television is about (and how it will change television viewing), will be dealt with later in the book. The single most important element which unites them is that the investment in and launch of digital television was a bet on two things:

- That television could move into markets and areas with which it had not formerly been associated.

■ That the viewers would gain more control over what they saw, how they saw it and how they paid for it. Television services that did not provide this would lose competitive advantage.

As with all technological revolutions, I believe that the implications and long term consequences of all this will be somewhat different – leading eventually to the demise of television viewing as it occurs now. Again, that is for a much later chapter.

How digital works

To understand the impact of digital it is necessary to understand something about its technology. However, to be blunt, there is no technology in the history of business which ever flourished without bestowing benefits on both its users and its owners. By and large, therefore, this is what this book will examine – as without these benefits the technology will not be with us for very long.

Most explanations of digital disappear fast into gobbledegook about 0s and 1s. That may be something that satisfies mathematicians but it is a very very abstract way of describing digital technology. This explanation deals with it from the point of view of television engineering, and how digital transforms it.

Analogue television generated scarcity – and scarcity was its handmaiden even in multichannel television. Multichannel simply overcame the problem of the amount of bandwidth taken by analogue signals by providing shedloads of bandwidth – either through fibre optic cables (in the case of cable television) or through satellite transponders (which are able to beam many many signals at a specific area of the earth's surface).

Digital transmission kills scarcity. This single fact is the first and most profound impact it has on television technology. It does this by ditching the way in which analogue sends pictures down a wire or through the airwaves.

Analogue transmission divides a picture into an image which can be drawn onto your television screen. So does digital – but in a radically different way. In analogue, the picture is captured by sweeping across it in a series of lines and then transmitting the lines as a continuous stream in the airwaves (Figure 1.2). The TV is told where to break the continuous line which it has been sent into individual lines, put them on top of one another, and so

Figure 1.2. Analogue screen image

assemble a picture. US analogue systems built pictures out of 525 lines – most European systems built a picture out of 625 lines.

Early analogue systems (in the 1930s) swept across the image formed by the camera lens using a mechanical system – a hole in a rotating disc. It was as simple as that. By the 1960s this was all done electronically – but the principle was the same: turning the picture into a series of lines, which were always analogous to the shape and intensity of the image.

The disadvantage of this system is that you have to transmit all of the image all of the time, even if the image itself is unchanged (for example, a testcard). It means that all available spectrum is always used in order to get any image, however complex or simple, to the TV screen.

Digital is simply a far more intelligent way of carrying images. In digital technology the camera's image is divided up into very small squares ('pixels' as they are called). Images are analysed as about a quarter of a million of these pixels in each picture. But in digital transmission, if there is no change in pixel from one television image to the next the transmission system does not

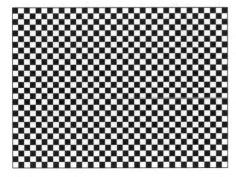

Figure 1.3. Digital screen image

bother to send any more information about that pixel – and the set top box understands that it gives that pixel the same value that it had last time.

The practical effect of this is that the signal can easily be reduced into a code which the receiving equipment understands – and being computer code it occupies far less bandwidth than the great motorways carved through the spectrum by analogue transmissions. It consists of all those 0s and 1s.

Digital transmission could not exist without computer technology's main asset – *its ability to make thousands of calculations a second*. It takes a microprocessor capable of analysing and encoding 25 quarter-million pixels images a second (and a receiver at the other end in your set top box disentangling them at the same rate) to make the system work. In other words, digital transmission could not have been made to work before there were commercially available microprocessors capable of making those many calculations at that speed. This was not possible before the 1990s – and that is why digital transmission did not really appear as a mass medium until 1995.

The first benefit of this development is that spectrum scarcity becomes history. It only takes a fraction of the satellite capacity required by analogue, for example, to beam down a television channel. The carrying capacity of the BSkyB system in the UK has gone from fifty channels to over seven hundred. Potentially, refining the satellite technology will double this. The carrying capacity of cable systems becomes virtually infinite with the right equipment at each end of the cable.

SLEEPING WITH THE ENEMY

However, in adopting this approach to transmission (in exchange for many potential business benefits) television has allowed a host of formidable adversaries into its citadel. Television's worst legacy is its history of effortless success. Everyone would like a part of it, as they perceive television to be the path to marketing supremacy and easy profit margins.

Digital development's main consequence is to give a host of wannabe communicators a path to television's audiences. The reason is that digital transmission, in reducing television to a sequence of computer data, has meant that television is now in the domain of computer technology. And the computer industry is a wild world.

- It is virtually unregulated – and most attempts to regulate it fail (the most recent example is Microsoft's escape from anti-trust burdens).
- It moves fast, and constantly invents new forms of content and ways of delivering that content.
- It is the preserve of the young – who for most advertisers are television's most important audience. The young have little attachment to old forms of transmission, are fascinated by the new and are immensely disloyal to the electronic past.

The significance of this last point can't be stressed enough – and will be a constant theme in this book.

Regulatory confusion

Television broadcasters carp about regulators – but in many ways the two have a symbiotic relationship. They need each other to justify what they do and the way in which they do it. Most importantly, they need each other to keep industries clearly defined. One of the unintended effects of regulation has been to preserve the sanctity of television as a distinct and separate medium. Digital demolishes this.

In a recent speech, the Chairman[5] of America's Federal Communications Commission summarises it in this way:

> If you use co-axial cable [cable television] and you provide a video service, you're called a cable service provider and Title VI controls what happens to you. If you use the airwaves to provide video images you're a broadcaster and Title III provides the rules for you. And if you're an information service provider or an Internet company, we love you so much, because that's our 'techno-ecstasy' thing. There are no rules for you – you're just kissed and blessed and sent into the world.
>
> But what happens when AT & T uses the same infrastructure to provide telephone service, video service and Internet service? They want to be called 'information service providers'. So the regulatory buckets that guide us, or are supposed to, are becoming increasingly irrational, arbitrary and difficult to apply.

This is more than just a regulator complaining that technology has overtaken him. His point is that he can't define who is in which markets anymore, nor which content should have which rules applied to it. Michael Porter[6] has a model which analyses competition, seeing new entrants to a market as a significant pressure and also as substitutes for the existing technology. It is very unusual in a market for both new entrants and substitutes to be impacting on an industry at the same time. But that is what is happening in the television industry right now. Markets are converging so fast that it is impossible to say what industry will emerge from the chaos. That is the side-effect of television adopting computer based transmission systems. It is a side-effect which will definitely alter the balance of the patient's behaviour.

Buying by return

A very important feature of digital broadcasting is that it allows viewers to buy through the television. Analogue could achieve this but it was technically very messy, requiring viewers to use their telephone to give their credit card details.

But with digital technology everything needed to make a purchase can be packaged together in the remote programme control. This can make the decision to buy almost an 'impulse' purchase – much loved by retailers as people are more likely to do it with little or no thought. A digital television system can provide this as it can monitor who you are, check your credit limit and allow you to buy – all through pressing keys on the television.

It does this by making use of a computer device called a 'return line'. Return lines are essential to the Internet as they allow users to send short messages to a remote store of content, which then sends your computer the content you want to see.

In digital cable systems, return lines pose no problems as they simply race back up the cable which is bringing the television pictures into your home. In satellite it is more of a problem, as it would be very expensive to allow users to send signals back up to the satellite. So satellite systems use the existing telephone network to give their viewers a return line. It dials into a special number of the platform owner and talks to the play out centre and (usually) to its credit control facility.

The disadvantage is that viewers normally need encouragement (or coercion) to connect a satellite box into a telephone line. As selling extra movies and services is an important extra source of revenue for digital TV operators (and one of the main reasons they invested in all the technology in the first place) platforms are keen to use the carrot and the stick. So BSkyB came up with a deal where you would get your set top box for free, on the understanding that you had to plug it into a telephone point for at least the first year. Not coming up with such a deal is cited as one of the reasons that the Kirch Pay TV system in Germany moved towards bankruptcy so fast.

However, return paths – once viewers are hooked into them – give digital television a whole extra dimension lacking from analogue. Viewers can:

- Pay for events or movies which the conditional access system then allows them to view
- Play games on the TV
- Vote on panels or in polls related to TV programming
- Buy objects they see on the TV direct through the TV
- Access the Internet
- Send and receive e-mails.

The return path (Figure 1.4) is the feature which is most convergent with computer technology – and also with direct customer relationship management.

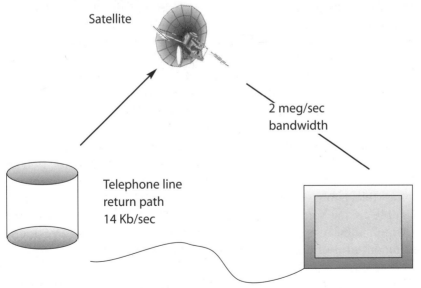

Satellite

2 meg/sec
bandwidth

Telephone line
return path
14 Kb/sec

Figure 1.4. A satellite return path

Customer relationship management is something at which analogue television was very bad. The networks, if they had any kind of information about their viewers, got them through surveys of what they thought of programmes. This created a distance between network and viewer which wasn't entirely healthy.

However, all viewers of digital TV platforms are subscribers (whether they pay a subscription or not[7]), and their records have to be kept on a computer system. Also, when they start to use the return path, platforms can track their actions and purchases.

This is the first time broadcasters have had such a direct relationship with their viewers. The science of instant viewer tracking is very much in its infancy. However, most suppliers of important digital channels admit that they have written into their contract with broadcast platforms that they have rights of access to subscriber information. How they use it and what they do with it, particularly when it comes to commissioning new programming, is an emerging science.

THE CHANGE IT HAD TO COME

Even the greatest technology in the world doesn't get adopted if no-one finds it useful or relevant. While it is possible to see benefits in digital technology for many groups, the ones for whom it seems natural – and who are gobbling up almost anything into which digital metamorphoses – are the 16–24 year olds.

MTV, more than any other television brand, owns this age segment. Other broadcasters cast envious eyes over MTV's supremacy in this area, as the 16–24 year olds are the Holy Grail of broadcasters. Get them at that age and television executives (and television advertisers) believe, like the Jesuits, they have them for life. This may or may not be true. However, what *is* true is the 16–24 year olds have been the most enthusiastic adopters of digital television. Because they are the rising generation, it is possible to see something of the future of television from the way in which they use the new medium. Sumner Redstone, President of Viacom and of its subsidiary MTV puts it like this:

For Viacom, the proliferation of platforms for interactive content – cell phones, the Internet and increasingly interactive PC broadband – is particularly potent. Our viewers are already on those platforms . . . in massive numbers. They're online: more than 60 per cent of MTV's international audience surf the web. Our viewers watch more television than their parents and, according to our research, they are multi-tasking as they do so, using all these media simultaneously. They are surfing the web, chatting with friends and receiving text messages on their cell phones as well as watching their favourite TV shows. MTV intends to get its brand in front of them, wherever they may be.[8]

Viacom's strategy to keep pace with the frenetic demand of its audience for new digital media, some of it not traditionally associated with television, is not merely to innovate in content but also to innovate in media:

Our leadership in exploiting new technologies . . . [has] led us to form 'content labs' – where our local teams innovate novel forms of content based on the latest technologies in their markets . . . The content we're creating for all of these new platforms is not about re-purposing content. MTV Live, for instance, was created specifically for PC broadband and is our response to an insatiable appetite for next-generation, interactive entertainment . . . To get in front of viewers who see their cell phones as the world's best communications device, MTV launched *Videoclash* in the UK in February. A fast-moving, visually stimulating show, viewers choose their favourite videos via text messages from their cell phones or the MTV UK Web site. There are no presenters. Instead videos, text from viewers and voice-overs drive the show.[9]

This thrust into many different forms of digital media – allied with an equally desperate need to tie them all together in a series of wild and unexpected combinations – is what Viacom believes it needs to do to keep its precious audiences' tiny attention span. But if that is the way the viewer of tomorrow behaves, that is what they will have to do to hang onto them.

So the fragmenting nature of television – and the way it flows in and out of new forms of communication – seems seamlessly joined to the fragmenting tastes and attention span of a new multi-tasking audience. An exact match between the needs of a new generation and a brand new technology are a very powerful and irresistible combination. They are sure to change fundamentally what we understand by the word 'television', and what it will stand for in ten years time.

This raises profound issues and problems for the people who run television – and the people who run its potent companion, television advertising. They need to know what is likely to happen: what strategies will win in the new television world and which will fail. That is what this book is about.

A model of television change

Figure 1.5 summarises the main elements of the evolution of television as it moves into digital transmission.

Television in the 1950s and 1960s was transmitted from masts using analogue technology. This made television transmission an activity dominated by spectrum scarcity and led inevitably to television monopolies. These monopolies took the form of channels which were so monopolistic that they could support themselves on one type of income alone: advertising.

The advent of analogue cable and satellite transmission meant that it was possible to create new networks which weakened the old terrestrial monopolies. Most importantly, it was possible to create *global* networks. These meant that channels transmitting to minority interests – such as business people, news junkies or 16–24 year olds – could survive. Multichannel meant that television began to develop more types of revenue source – including subscriber income – as well as advertising.

The switch from analogue to digital completely disrupts both the technology and the nature of television. With digital, there is little distinction between the way in which television is transmitted and that in which *other* forms of data are transmitted. This means that the difference between television content and other content begins to blur. If MTV allows viewers to vote via SMS text on the outcome of a television show, then what is television? This book sees this as the start of the death of the television channel, and the beginning of the rise of companies which specialise in branded electronic content. But the change is even more fundamental and far-reaching than that. That is for later chapters.

All this has a profound impact on the economics of television, and how money is made (and lost) in the television industry.

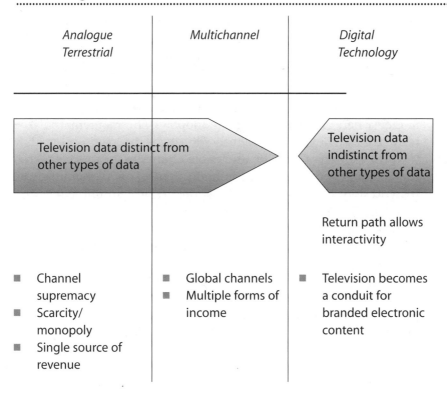

Figure 1.5. Television change model

Changes in the economics of television

In retrospect, what is strange about the television industry is that it enjoyed such a long period during which the forces of technological change were held in check. Such changes that took place in its first forty years – like the arrival of colour in the 1960s – had almost no impact on the fundamental television business environment.[10]

The single sudden change which is so profoundly shocking to broadcasters is the simple fact that television is no longer 'a licence to print money'.[11] At the time of writing you have to be located slightly 'outside' television to appreciate this, or at least not brought up entirely within it. Matthew Symonds[12] came to television from setting up one of the new UK newspapers (*The Independent*) which took advantage of the lower costs which technological change could bring to newspaper production. He then became

Director of Strategy for the commercial arm of the BBC, where he had to consider what parts of television – if any – were still profitable. Ask him if television is a licence to print money any more and he pauses, says 'that's a good question', and then replies:

> No, I don't think it is. I think you only have a licence to print money when you have a near-monopoly. The moment that the terrestrial analogue monopolies were broken down – obviously with the launch of satellite and cable channels – it was clear that the economics of the business had to change very significantly. It's certainly the case that the economics of running cable and satellite channels are very far from being a licence to print money. They are actually very scary. You have to find ways of surviving on audience shares of 0.2 per cent. So, first of all, you know you're not going to make any money for years. You're going to have to keep your costs under extraordinarily tight control. You're going to have to be very smart about where you get your programmes from. Probably in a market the size of the UK, for example, there will only be ten or twelve channels, which will be good businesses when we have full penetration of digital receivers.

In the UK the first and most profound effect of changing television technology has been the decline in ITV's audience share. In 1994, ITV still boasted a 40 per cent share of all of the UK audience. However, by late 2001 this had slipped to 25 per cent. Most viewers have escaped to new non-terrestrial channels, distributed by cable or to satellite. These non-terrestrial channels by late 2001 had 22 per cent of the audience. Although no single channel there has a share to rival one of the old terrestrial channels, the cumulative effect has been devastating.

In the UK 1998 also saw the launch of ONdigital, which transmits multichannel television over fixed masts. The combined impact of this, digital cable and SkyDigital has been to increase the number of households receiving digital television to 7.8 million – about 31 per cent of UK households. This represents an increase, over two years, from 12 per cent of households. In other words, in the space of two years the number of households receiving digital television in the UK has almost tripled.

Digital has destroyed ITV's hold of on the UK market. Traditional broadcasters have been incredulous at the speed of its demise.

However, this situation also makes the UK an exciting testbed for the future of digital television. While the USA has highly developed cable systems, it has still not made the leap straight to digital technology seen in the UK.

The ascendancy of digital involves conundrums and shocks for broadcasters. In the UK this manifests itself vividly at the dinners held by the Royal Television Society, at which producers and executives can voice their opinions. A very distinguished producer of situation comedy announced there that she couldn't understand why, with the massive expansion of airtime, channels were offering less and less money for new programmes. 'Surely', she said, 'the more television there is, there have to be more people to pay for it?'

Old ways of doing business always die slowest in the minds of traders who have seen no change in their business for many years. They view change as a violation of a rule of nature. Television practitioners will have the biggest problems of all because their stable, predictable and rich industry has been invaded by the fastest moving technology on earth – computer technology – which is now calling into question the security of their comfortable habitat. In many ways digital creates a wrenching psychological clash – between an old cultural elite and a very young innovative technology, which cares little for labels such as 'quality' or 'balance' but simply seeks expanding markets. However, it is only clear to a few far-sighted operators what form the new technologies and the new programming will take. So most people in the old elite have no answers – and the new elite is making content which no one currently recognises as television. The old is dying and the new has yet to be born. In this kind of situation many extraordinary things occur, and ideas and values are challenged unscrupulously.

This book will look at the five issues for which broadcasters have the fewest answers. These are examined in detail in Chapter 2. Until the fog over the future of television clears, these will remain the main headaches at the back of broadcasters' minds. It will then reveal the strategies which are most likely to succeed – taking best practice from broadcasters who have thought about the competitive advantage offered by digital and are exploiting it.

Even some of the newest strategies, like platform ownership, seem questionable when their economics are examined. A stark question remains: would some of today's broadcasters be better off selling up and giving up? It is, after all, rarely the existing large players who profit from rapid technological change. Ask NCR, IBM or Marconi.

The issues examined in the next chapters are as follows:

2. A view of the new viewer

In the UK, migration of viewers from traditional to digital viewing occurred rapidly. This is a very worrying phenomenon for UK broadcasters, as they watch television channels which are alleged to contain the 'highest quality programmes in the world' losing their market share as viewers migrate wholesale to other channels available over digital. So what has driven this change? Why have the audiences become so fickle? Why, indeed, are they willing to take out monthly subscriptions which are far higher than anything they have previously been prepared to pay for television content?

In Italy, the change to digital viewing actually seems to have arrested while the terrestrial networks still hold large market shares. This could be because in Italy the biggest commercial television operator and the Prime Minister are the same person.

Also, what is happening, and what is likely to happen in future, in the biggest television market in the world – the USA? Will the move to digital television there be as rapid there as it has been in the UK?

3. Channel wars

Many existing players have tried to maintain their audience share by creating new channels. This has led to unprecedented costs, as the new channels absorb increasing amounts of money on the way to breaking even. So far, only Disney and MTV have managed to make this strategy work. The rest, including Channel 4, have sustained appalling losses. What makes the difference between success and failure in creating digital channels?

4. The peculiar rise and fall of the platform owners

Platform owners are a new phenomenon. Terrestrial broad-casting involved no direct relationship with the viewers as the television signal, dispersed from transmission masts, was free to air. However with the advent of multi-channel TV, which required encryption via a set top box, a new breed of television traders has appeared: the platform owner. They supply a set top box to the viewer (in the UK for no charge) in order that the viewer can subscribe to a multi-channel offering. However, this also means that from now on the broadcaster and the viewer have a far closer relationship. As the platform owners levy a subscription on the viewer, they need details of bank account, address and even creditworthiness. This is information which terrestrial commercial television can only dream about. In addition, the viewers give away details of their viewing habits direct to the platform owner through the set top box, and the platform owner may interrogate it.

In the late nineties this situation appeared to give the platform owners an unassailable position, as they could monitor the habits of the viewer so closely that they would be able to predict future viewing trends and commission accordingly. But this enviable future perfect doesn't seem to have made the present tense. The platform owners have been beset by increasing and uncontrollable costs from programme makers, and by fierce competition from alternative platforms. This chapter looks at what has gone wrong with the 'winning strategy' of platform owning.

5. Making production pay

There is now greater pressure to judge the right content for a television audience than ever before. This is because getting it wrong costs money which television companies simply don't have. No producer has a right to fail any more – a right that some certainly used to enjoy.

The best kind of content is the 'hit' – something which an audience feels they *must* watch. Sometimes these occur almost by accident (like *Who Wants To Be A Millionaire*), sometimes by design (like *Friends*). Companies like Disney which are heavily skewed towards television production spend a great deal of time trying to work out the next hit. They have refined their production process so they can intervene the second that they know something is going off-course, and correct or kill it. As Michael Eisner, Chief Executive of Walt Disney, says: 'We are a company that only succeeds or fails on the quality of its products'.[13]

Are these new production techniques effective? And what kind of television do they generate? Does it produce more hits or more homogeneity?

6. Watch out America: you're next!

Digital broadcasting still has a significantly lower penetration in the States than in Europe, where in the UK and France it reaches 39 per cent of television households. Europe has been making the running (and making the mistakes) necessary to establish what works and what fails in digital broadcasting.

US television stations have been reluctant to embrace digital technology because it is expensive to install and because multi-channel television is received by 95 per cent of US households. However there are compelling reasons why America will have to switch rapidly to digital in order to keep up with the demands of the new television audience.

Two of the most important lessons for broadcasters to learn are to stop trying to appeal to a mass audience and to stop trying to make hit shows. These will prove hard habits to kick – but they are expensive and wasteful habits which must be jettisoned soon.

Broadcasters need to understand that the reasons which the affluent had for adopting digital television will be eclipsed by the reasons why the young rely on it. The young use digital television as part of a 'media motorway' supporting and enhancing their lifestyle. Irrationally, the young believe that there are severe constraints on their time – and are impatient with systems which can't save them time. They also look to media to put them in touch with their 'community' – the group with whom they identify and from whom they draw their opinions.

No technology or society can now resist the demands of the next generation of television viewers – not even America.

7. The commercial breaks

The most profound questions which the changes in television raise are for the advertising industry. The basic business model in advertising is beguilingly simple: clients pay an agency a percent-age of the total spent by the client on a campaign, typically about 15 per cent. This gives advertisers an incentive to find expensive places to advertise – to date, television has been the answer to their prayers. In fact about 60 per cent of the money spent in a typical campaign is on television advertising. Clients could be persuaded to do this as it was always argued that television could deliver a mass audience.

But this is no longer true. So clients have started to ask how they can reach their target customers using a medium that is fragmenting. Clients have also started to ask why terrestrial television advertising is so expensive. So advertisers are having to ask themselves who should advertise on television, and how. One of the effects of the collapse in ITV audience share has been the migration of campaigns to other channels where airtime is cheaper. Nick Milligan, Deputy CEO of the UK's Channel 5, says that 'television advertising is approaching 1998 prices. It's incredibly good value and we should see new market sectors using the medium for the first time'.[14]

This is all very disturbing for the advertising industry, however. If the price of advertising is getting cheaper, how will agencies survive? Worse, the type of advertising is changing. Digital television offers interactive forms of advertising, which have worked well in France and are only starting to be used in the UK and America. How will the industry adapt to targeting smaller and more specialised audiences using new and unfamiliar media – and all for less money?

8. Finding business models that work

One little-noticed impact of multichannel television was that it challenged television's basic business model – in other words, the way in which television managed to make a profit. Whereas terrestrial television has always relied predominantly on advertising for its revenue, multichannel television found out quickly that this would not work when there were thirty or more television channels.

So multichannel television has always relied for the majority of its revenues on subscription – the monthly figure which any subscriber to a multichannel platform is prepared to pay for a 'bundle' of channels. A proportion of this is held by the platform provider and a proportion is handed on to the supplier of the channel. Consequently, success and failure for new digital channels is often determined by the amount of subscription revenue the channel provider has managed to get from the platform operator.

It also has strange consequences. For example, in a recession subscription-based television tends to do well and the old advertising-based terrestrial channels do badly. This is thought to happen because people watch more television during a recession – and are reluctant to give up their subscriptions to multichannel. Advertisers' clients cut back on advertising, however, so terrestrial channels suffer.

But the new technology which is now impacting on the television market could – and should – produce even more television business models. However, it is remarkable how little experimentation there has been in the television industry. Katherine Everett, Director of Interactive for the BBC, famously replied to the question 'How do you make money out of interactive TV?' with 'Search me'.

This chapter will examine new business models that are likely to be tried as broadcasters become more daring with new television technology.

9. Killer operators

This chapter is about who is likely to win the technology war in digital television, and why. Getting the technology correct is essential as it is part and parcel of an operator's business model. Get the wrong technology and you will not meet the high demands of the new audience. Some strategies are already clearly more likely to succeed than others are – and to capture the lion's share of the fickle multi-tasking audience with which all media owners must cope in the future.

The next generation of set top boxes will allow viewers to escape adverts entirely – and evidence suggests that advertisers will lose 70 per cent of their viewers this way. Those who have the right technology in place to deal with the collapse of the commercial break will emerge with a huge advantage.

The pace of change in digital is so rapid that many existing broadcasters are likely to disappear rapidly. From the players' characteristics it will be clear who will be the losers.

10. The end of the beginning

The new digital format of the television industry will have profound consequences for a society in which television is the most important medium of communication. This chapter deals with what the new television will mean for politics, democracy and the way we think and feel.

A View of the New Viewer

THE FASTEST GROWING ELECTRONIC MEDIUM OF ALL TIME ISN'T TELEVISION

The most worrying phenomenon for the television industry was the growth of the Internet – which really began to stand on its tail and expand in the mid 1990s. Worrying because there is one statistic about the Internet which urgently needs explanation and yet which has never been fully researched: 'why did it take off so fast?' In North America it reached a penetration of 50 million users in just five years – whereas TV took twenty years and radio about forty. So what has the Internet got which TV hasn't? Surely the Internet, unlike television, is dismally disadvantaged by not having full screen moving pictures?

The Internet's earliest adopters were the affluent – the ABs (using the ACORN classification). Why did the affluent, who watch the least television, go for the Internet when it was a difficult and immature medium in the nineties? The truth is that no one really knows the answer, but a logical hypothesis is that the ABs simply ran out of time.

Time used to be in abundant supply in Western society. In some places it still is, as anyone doing business with France will testify. However, in Anglo/American Society in particular some disturbing things were happening to the affluent. The most obvious is that people in the modern office are generally better off than their predecessors of thirty years ago – but have less time at their disposal. Although the economic slowdown has meant that some have enforced leisure, those still in the market are working hard at new business pitches attempting to make the work come through. When asked who they compare their own performance to, and the performance of their company, they usually mention one of the world's big service industry players – Citicorp, or Price Waterhouse Coopers or Axa (in insurance). The point is that, unlike the 1970s office workers, they are no longer competing with the company down the road. They are competing with global companies, and the stiffness of the competition is determined by what these global players are doing across many countries.

The reason that we now compete in international marketplaces is the spread of networks carrying vast amounts of data around the world. The spread of data networks, and their effect on how we live and work, is one of the great under-researched topics of our generation. Their practical effect has meant that it is possible for us to deal with and compete with companies located in another place and another time zone. We used to do this by phone – but the phone is only as effective as the individuals you can gather together on the end of it. The real power is in data lines linking machines, which do not need people to be together at the same time and can be used to close deals (if the dealing is as simple as trading stock).

Interestingly, the statistics support this view. Worldwide data traffic easily surpasses voice traffic in terms of volume. International Data Corp. (IDC) estimates that the number of people using the Internet surpassed 500 million in 2001, and may reach almost a billion by 2005. Total bandwidth demand is expected to grow at a compound annual rate of 70 per cent between now and 2005.[15]

The point is that people need more and smarter data in order to compete in a global environment – and more and smarter access to markets. That is what the Internet provides. To cope with being time- and competition-pressured people have had to work smarter – and that has meant the growth of anything which can link, provide information, make deals and analyse. In these circumstances, the Internet took off like a rocket. It was the perfect medium for the time-pressured who found themselves stuck in fierce competitive crossfire. They chose the Internet because it deals in *interactive global data*. Television, in the 1990s, remained national, one-way, and wedded to one form of data: television pictures.

SMART VIEWING

So how do these changes in the way people work affect the way in which they consume television? *The problem for the broadcasting industry is that the people who use screens at work to 'work smart' will come home and demand to 'view smart' as well.* Many US broadcasters in particular doubt this – as is evidenced in the reluctance of small US stations to convert to digital transmission. Others dismiss the 'smart viewing' proposition as not applicable to television since people use television in a different way from a personal computer. At the PC, you 'lean forward' and are actively engaged in hitting the keys and talking to the machine. With a television you 'lean back' – it is primarily an entertainment medium and you do not want to interact so much. A strong exponent of this distinction is Andy Grove, the President of Intel Corp.

However, this neglects the fact that people do not change the way they view the world simply because they have come home from work. This is exactly what happened in the UK with the launch of SkyDigital, for which critics said there would be no demand because everyone had enough television channels already. But what happened in reality is that as soon as viewers realised that movies and events could be received and re-scheduled virtually on demand, as if you were buying television programmes in a supermarket, they made it the fastest growing service in British television history.

The fact is that people adapt, and consequently change the way in which they view the world. They also change the way in which they view television. One of the most interesting pieces of research to come out of social researchers at The Henley Centre in recent years is that the people best equipped to overcome stress in 2002 are now Americans. Having invented it, they have simply evolved and adapted, either by changing their lifestyle and no longer doing 9–5 office hours or by 'living smarter' – that is, using technology to assist them and make them more productive.

This is what is happening in entertainment and television consumption. People won't compromise with a channel schedule which presents them with something they don't like anymore. They will watch 'exactly what they want when they want it'. In other words, they behave in front of the television exactly the way in which they do at work – although they lean back when they are doing it. They make the same stringent demands of an electronic provider of entertainment as they do of their supermarket or online bookstore.

In this way the coming of digital television – and its take-up – has become inevitable.

THE FOUR TRIBES

There are really four main tribes of television consumers:

- The affluent
- The high consumers
- Those indifferent to digital
- The young.

One of these tribes is likely to turn the whole way in which television is consumed so upside-down that none of us now living will recognise it. However, the basic attitudes of the tribes are as follows:

1. The affluent

The important point about the affluent is that they are the people driven simultaneously by the new economy into both affluence and lack of time. They need new ways of working and living smarter, so they constantly seek them out. Digital television seems to offer more efficient use of their television time – so they are they first to buy it. Not for them the wait through soap operas for the drama they want to see. They go straight for their drama on demand. Not for them choice – choice takes too much time. They demand exactly what they want when they want it. Digital television is their natural medium and they are the first to adopt it.

Yet the affluent now have a new role. They are the platform owners' secret weapon and secret hope. The platform owners control the direct paying relationship with the viewer (see Chapter 4). But there comes a point where the economics of digital transmission mean that platform owners – be they on satellite, cable, terrestrial or broadband – need to increase their revenues rather than increase their share and get into profit. They do this by targeting the affluent viewers. Peter Bazalgette, Chairman of Dutch-owned production house Endemol UK,[16] describes it like this:

> I estimate that affluent individual consumers of media will spend 50 per cent more on media in the next ten years. So that is why Tony Ball's plan at BSkyB is that he's got 5.9 million subscribers at the moment and he doesn't particularly want to grow that number to 7 million. He wants his 5.9 million to spend £500 a year

rather than £300, and that is what he is really concentrating on. He doesn't want another 3 million of the impoverished spending £180 a year from the wreck of ITV Digital. He wants high rollers.[17]

The affluent, who were the first to migrate to digital television, are therefore also the first who will bring it into profit. That is why, despite the sometimes downmarket reputation of multichannel television, digital television is going to contain a lot of upmarket programming. It needs to so that affluent viewers spend more on it. That is hard business logic.

2. The high consumers

The high consumers are vital in the initial battle for share in the digital television market place. Although they are not affluent, they are prepared to spend a disproportionate amount of their wages on television. In the early days of a platform it is important to build up a lot of them, as it increases share to a point where you can claim higher audiences – and so charge premium rates for advertising, drive harder deals with channel and content owners and see off the competition. But the cost of acquiring and retaining them is high. BSkyB, from the launch of SkyDigital, gave away its set boxes for free (with certain conditions attached[18]). This had the triple effect of:

- Drawing in the high television consumers
- Forcing competitors to do the same
- Forcing people to connect set top boxes to a telephone line (a condition for receiving a free box).

Operators who didn't give away free set top boxes, like Kirch Media in Germany, never got a large enough critical mass of viewers to make their heavy investments in content worthwhile. However being on the receiving end of a competitor who is out to corner the market in high television consumers is an uncomfortable experience. Stuart Prebble, the former CEO of failed digital platform ITV Digital, says that when SkyDigital started to give away free set top boxes, 'ITV Digital had a clear choice to follow their lead, or to throw in the towel. The decision to follow effectively doubled the peak funding requirements of the business.'[19]

But when a platform has reached a critical mass of subscribers it needs to switch its loyalties to the affluent. Informa Media Group has SkyDigital subscribers growing by only 1.5 million between 2002 and 2010 – but has the annual revenues per subscriber growing from £336 to £410.[20]

3. Those indifferent to digital

The Informa Media Group estimates also show only 65 per cent of UK households subscribing to digital television by 2010. Currently 39 per cent subscribe via satellite, cable or terrestrial. This is far short of the Government's ideal of 95 per cent. Governments are keen on a total migration to digital from analogue, as it allows the terrestrial spectrum freed up by the introduction of digital to be sold off.

Figures in the US tend to support the idea that multichannel television is a big enough draw to get viewers over to digital. In the US over 90 per cent of households have multichannel television.[21] However, only a small proportion of these are digital as the digital roll-out is much slower. Americans also seem to have a much higher tolerance of low-quality pictures and lack of interactivity. In the latter case, this is probably because of the very high rate of Internet penetration (60 per cent). But it took the US over twenty years to achieve this – and most of Europe has only had multi-channel for about ten years. Europe also migrated to digital trans-mission faster because it was the fastest way to upgrade existing transmission systems.

However, European audiences are all used to a strong tradition of public service broadcasting which means that they are used to a lot of content being free at the point of delivery. Many people who still receive a lot of original and expensive programming with ordi-nary analogue reception equipment resent paying £30/month for additional, less well-funded television channels. In Northern Europe this is thought to apply to over 40 per cent of households. In Italy multichannel television has struggled to reach even 20 per cent of households, but this is because the standard terrestrial broadcasters are well funded and have the total support of the government. The biggest commercial television magnate in Italy, Silvio Berlusconi, is also currently Prime Minister.

So there is a large 'indifferent to digital' mountain to overcome in Europe. In the US it is less of an obstacle, as multichannel house-holds will inevitably switch to digital as broadcasters upgrade. Digital will offer the consumer exactly what they want when they want it – an idea which will be irresistible in American society. The main barrier to the spread of digital transmission in the US at present is the reluctance of broadcasters to pay for the upgrade. Broadcasters say it costs from $2 million to $10 million to upgrade a station. However, the Federal Communications Commission requires all broadcasters to transmit digitally in the US by 2006, although 894 out of 1,315 commercial stations facing the deadline have asked for a six-month extension.[22]

In Europe, some new way of paying for digital will have to be found to entice viewers away from analogue transmission. The most likely solution will be that digital terrestrial transmission systems, which have so far proved unable to make a profit, will be gifted in some way to publicly funded broadcasters. This has happened now in the UK, with viewers able to receive all of the existing free to air channels – plus some of the free to air channels only available on digital television – through a one-off purchase of a set top box (possibly about $50). The argument is that since the taxpayer is paying for all the European free to air public service channels anyway, why shouldn't they be able to receive them? The barrier to this solution is that many European publicly funded broadcasters are barred from going into pay television. However, the desperation of the governments of Spain, the UK and Sweden to make a success of digital terrestrial may mean that the broadcasting licences of the state broadcasters are bent to allow this to happen. No one ever claimed that state broadcasting was about free competition, after all. It is about maintaining the 'quality' of national broadcasting, whatever that means.

So those indifferent to digital remain a bigger problem in Europe than in the US – even though the US has digitised less of its transmission infrastructure.

The young

The group which makes the future of television very hard to call is the young. Presented with digital technology, the young have started to use it in ways that would never have occurred to previous generations. Several themes are emerging about their viewing habits. They are:

■   Promiscuous in their viewing, and don't stick to television schedules

- Prepared to watch several media simultaneously
- Attracted by something in which they can be actively involved electronically
- More trusting of their leaders than they are of any communications or other medium
- Prepared to steal content – and to pass it on.

Peter Bazalgette has to monitor the way in which 10–24 year olds are viewing new media as it affects the way he makes his programmes. He starts his research at home, by watching his own children. He also has the next generation of technology at home: in this case the TiVo set top box. The TiVo (which is dealt with in more detail in Chapter 4) records the output of all the channels on digital television simultaneously and then gives the viewer the ability to retrieve and play any programme over the last week. He is fascinated by what happens when you place new technology in front of an audience who have no preconceptions about how television ought to be consumed:

> The first thing is that choice has led to promiscuity. There is no such thing as a schedule watched all the way through the evening by young people – and this is hugely significant in terms of whether channels will continue to exist in the future. It's also hugely significant in terms of even getting people to watch ads. And that's just what people do with their remote control – let alone the consequences of the electronic programmes guide.[23] Then if you have a house with a TiVo, as I have had for a year and a half, there are even more profound changes. I monitored my children's viewing over a week and they notched up 31 hours in aggregate between them – so fifteen hours each. More than a third was time-shifted, using the TiVo device. And they never watch ads when they time shift. Published TiVo statistics say this is true of over 70 per cent. This has profound implications for how we fund television and what the model is for advertising. And every advertising agency in the world is panicking. Simple consumer behaviour when presented with this technology is sending shock waves right through the system.

Advertisers tend to deny (publicly at least) that the young are ignoring channels and, even worse, ignoring conventional advertising. However, Bazalgette says that he has been approached by advertisers looking at new forms of television promotion that will appeal to the young – in his words, 'the advertisers are worried sick'. The young are an extremely important audience to advertisers simply because they are going to be around for a long time. Get them now and you may have them for life. But even if you got the young to watch something on the TV there is still a problem, as the way they consume media is profoundly different from that of their parents:

> Then when you add the PC. My boy very rarely has the TV on unless he's using the PC as well. So he's only giving the tele half his attention. On the one hand it says that here are two people, aged eleven and fifteen, using more media simultaneously than you or I every dreamt of. It actually means that individual users are going to spend more on their media.

This notion of impulse purchasing of media is very important to Bazalgette's thinking. He believes that the young, exposed to more media, will want to purchase more media from many more sources. There will almost certainly be the means for them to do so – with content arriving in the home from many different sources via many different conduits (see Chapter 4).

There is a flaw in this argument, however, which arises from the technical smartness of the young coupled with their lack of respect for intellectual property. It has started in the music industry, where new records are routinely downloaded off the Internet and burnt onto a CD using the recipient's computer. It does not take a very sophisticated computer to have these facilities. The International Federation of the Phonographic Industry says that demand for blank CD-Rs (recordable CDs) has risen two and half times from 1.9 billion units in 1999 to 4.8 billion in 2001. It estimates that at least half of these are used to record music, putting the number of illegal copies at 2.4 billion – which is equivalent to the size of legitimate record sales.[24]

In Germany, record sales fell by 11 per cent last year as a result of illegal duplication. In Italy 25 per cent of CDs are recorded off computer illegally. Interestingly, Italy also poses Canal Plus the biggest problems – with one third of its viewers receiving it using pirated access cards.

The implication for a burgeoning world of video content is clear: make sure it is secure or it will get copied, particularly by the young who have the technical skills and confidence. Only then may Peter Bazalgette's vision of more and more money being spent on electronic content be realised.

The tendency of the young to keep an eye on several programmes simultaneously has profound implications for television production. There is no point in screening a finely crafted documentary to this audience simply because it demands the viewer's undivided attention in order to be able to understand it. Already people's tendency to skip between media until they find something which attracts them has had an effect on programme structure:

> One of the interesting things is that television has to be cleverer. That's why the format has risen in popularity. A format is a higher concept than a documentary, with a bit more of a narrative to it. It's a fact that only a small part of entertainment is making people laugh – the main part is telling them stories. People like stories, so you hook them. The format is a type of plot. Why is history much to the fore, as Channel 4 and the Discovery Channel do it? They've rediscovered history because they've started telling narratives. One way of hooking people is to make programmes which have more of a narrative and an outcome to them.

There is a similar impact on advertisers, for whom simply holding the attention of the younger generation is a challenge. Rupert Howell, founder of advertising agency HHCL, puts it this way:

> There is a generation growing up now which is a headline generation – a soundbite generation – and I think increasingly the main payload of a piece of television advertising has to be pretty simple and direct. I think that we've got a generation coming through now which doesn't automatically get engaged in the message, and that it is perfectly natural to go through to a website for more information.

It is possible to engage the young more using the new technology. *Big Brother*, a programme which involves locking ten to twelve people up in a house for six weeks and observing their every move on television, managed to hit a rich seam with its use of interactivity. Every week, viewers vote on who should stay in the house and who should be evicted. This can be done by phone but increasingly it is done by pressing a button on the set top box controller, which sends a signal back to the broadcaster via a telephone line. The younger generation loves it:

> There are new techniques, like getting people to interact with a programme. People love taking part in *Big Brother*. They love affecting the outcome, and they love doing it because they are emotionally involved in *Big Brother*. *Big Brother*'s average audience of a night is 4 or 5 million. Its reach is 15 million. It had 17 or 18 million votes over both the series, with some people multiple voting. How many people actually voted? Probably about 7 or 8 million. BSkyB told us at the beginning of series two that we would get about 250,000 of these red button pushes on the controller (it was in effect a phone call). Well we got 5.5 million. That opened BSkyB's eyes to what interactivity can do. The process of giving people something they enjoy is one of binding people to the programme brand – if not the channel brand. And that's a new trick.

Rupert Howell says, rather optimistically, that his agency has discovered that the young are more suggestible if you get your message to people they trust – in particular their leaders and opinion formers. This may be because we now have a generation coming up which has a low attention span, likes smart gadgets and has no fixed political beliefs. In fact, they are not entirely sure what politics is for:

> 16–24 year olds are incredibly promiscuous, and I think the old idea that 'get 'em young and you've got them for life' is pretty much discredited. The answer is that while they are promiscuous and hard to nail down they are also very easily led. You only have to pick out the 10 per cent of opinion formers among 16–24 year olds and you've got them all. So you produce advertising, guerrilla marketing and all sorts of things which – while they appear to appeal to all 16–24 years – really target the 10 per cent of opinion leaders in that group. Once you've got them, you've got them all. If the leaders love the advertising, it gets talked about on the television and in the magazines. It's cheaper if you get it right quickly – but they are a hard group to nail down. Researching those groups is hard. Researchers go to bars and clubs; they do research on the Internet. What we do now is more difficult and complex – but it's just put a premium on the bits that we most enjoy and do best. It carries more risk and more reward.

A subtle but important message from observing the young using television is that they behave as if they don't have the time, even though youth is a period when time should not be in short supply. In other words they have begun to imitate the behaviour of the affluent, almost as a pose. This phenomenon has big implications for countries where digital television is about to go over the critical 33 per cent of television households mark, like the USA. The implications, and what it means for increasing audience share, will be dealt with in Chapter 5.

WHAT DOES IT MEAN?

The relationship between television and its audience is currently in complete flux. The way in which the various audiences view television content, and how they feel it should be consumed, are all up for grabs. However, it will have to be resolved – as an audience presented with a new technology will only use it in ways which offer clear benefits. Apart from the affluent, for whom the benefits are clear, the other three audiences are still experimenting with the new television technology and adapting it to their needs. For example, it is clear from SkyDigital's estimates of interactive participation in *Big Brother* and the actual take-up that the young had a far clearer idea of the benefits of that service than the broadcasters. In digital television, only the audience knows – and only the audience can tell you which technology is relevant to them.

The urgent demands of the various audiences mean there will be continuing changes in the following parts of the television world:

- Formats
- Advertising
- Interactivity
- The deal between the viewer and the distributor
- Security and access.

Formats

These have already changed, as Peter Bazalgette says when he talks about a lot of factual programming adopting almost a game show format. But they are likely to change even more. It is apparent that when a very popular show emerges which involves voting whether individual participants should stay on the show or not, the way in which that programme is screened will adapt to help viewers make more informed choices. *Big Brother* illustrates this – Channel 4 used an extra digital channel to screen continuous coverage of the *Big Brother* house and to allow viewers (and voters) to follow their favourite characters on individual cameras. Already the way in which the audience views and uses the medium is producing forms of television previously unknown.

Advertising

Advertising faces the biggest challenge. The demise of the habit of staying tuned continuously to a channel means that spot 30-second commercials are an endangered species. What takes their place is something closer to 'on demand' information, where details of products and how to order them through the TV are placed somewhere in the digital television set top box. However, advertisers will always tell you that 'if you want to tell someone a message first of all you have to attract their attention'. The single greatest challenge for television advertisers is to get the attention of the new, promiscuous programme-hopping viewer. This is dealt with in Chapter 7.

Interactivity

Peter Bazalgette is schizophrenic about interactivity. On one hand, he is justly proud of the way it is now an integral part of *Big Brother*; on the other, he reckons that no-one buys a digital platform because you can order a pizza from it – or look up your bank account (see interview in Chapter 8). He is probably right on both counts. It is simply that the *Big Brother* form of interactivity has found its audience and online pizza delivery hasn't. It may never do so.

The forms of interactivity that will succeed are likely to be related to programme content. In other words, the drivers of interactivity on digital TV will be the programmes, or video clips. They are what will attract attention and create an emotional bond with the audience. Interactivity that works will enhance or extend television material. The future does not look bright for interactive retailing, banking or other activities through the television that are not related in some way to a high profile programme which tugs at the emotions of its audience.

The deal between the viewer and the distributor

This is the area of most profound change. The technology enables the audience to make previously unheard-of demands of the broadcaster – which in digital television is likely to be the platform owner (see Chapter 4). Peter Bazalgette thinks that some audiences, perhaps the affluent, are likely to barter their attention in return for added benefits from the broadcaster:

> When BT did a video on demand trial they said, 'if you take ads we'll give you a lower subscription'. That discount is actually the price of the viewer's attention. What's happened with digital television is that the boot is now on the other foot. Rather than getting me to buy the television company's services, I'm actually selling them my attention. Now the consumer is boss. They're not being spoon-fed by channel controllers – they really are selling their attention. There's a completely different dynamic to old analogue television.

This is an area to which we will return in Chapter 10.

Security and access

There will not be continued growth in digital television revenues without increased and more sophisticated security and access. This is because of two pressures:

- The innate tendency of audiences (particularly the young) to pirate electronic content and digital access
- The need to charge on a pay per view basis to raise revenues per viewer: this can only be done with sophisticated electronic gateways.

BSkyB's latest revenues show that average annual revenue per subscriber has risen 11 per cent to £341 in 2001. Sky want to get revenues up to £400 per subscriber. That cannot be achieved without a watertight access system – which they have in place from NDS (see Chapter 9). However, the same goes for any broadcasters selling programmes to the public in the world of digital television. In the digital world the number of television outlets selling directly to the viewer is likely to increase, not decrease (see Chapter 10).

Channel Wars

SLASHING COSTS

Digital television opens the gates to newcomers to the TV industry. Newcomers who couldn't have afforded the only previous way of getting pictures to viewers: analogue transmission. This is the most threatening aspect of digital for existing operators. Existing networks are powerless to prevent new channels, often well funded by US broadcasters, starting up in their territory. In the US, channels run by people who have never previously been in broadcasting have been launched. For example, the Discovery Network was started by a former librarian. This is why some existing operators have started up new channels themselves as a means of self-defence.

Digital technology lowers both the transmission costs of television and the costs of actually running a channel. These two costs used to form significant barriers to starting television channels. It is six times more expensive to transmit a channel from a satellite using analogue technology than it is to use a digital signal.

There is also another hidden reason why digital transmission is so much cheaper. Digital fundamentally changes the way in which channels are managed and played out.

Figure 3.1 shows the television production chain. In the middle sits the difficult process of channel management. This consists of:

- Making sure all the tapes are present for a complete day's schedule
- That the tapes are all played out in the correct order
- That they are being played out without faults or glitches
- That a record is kept of what was played out, and for how long (for regulatory and rights purposes)
- That the adverts are inserted and played out in the right places, and a record is kept of what went out and when.

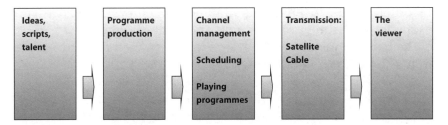

Figure 3.1. The television production chain

Analogue transmission – with all material kept on tape – meant that this process typically occupied eight people during the course of a day. At large networks it occupied even more people. In digital television this whole process occupies one person. In some multi-channel operations it takes even less.

This is because programme material in digital operations can be held and transmitted by computer. Tapes are no longer required, dramatically reducing the amount of manual intervention. Digital transmission can be computer controlled – and the programmes assembled, played out and monitored by a computer programme.

This is called *server-based transmission*. A server is a large computer data processor and store. Servers also hold web sites and can run software applications – so it is an easy step to combining e-commerce applications with television channels.

Lower the technical costs of playing out and transmitting a television channel and many channels become economically viable. The issue then becomes one of identifying what viewers, used to a diet of well-funded mass appeal channels, miss that will lure them away from the main networks.

This has led to a proliferation of 'themed' channels – that is, channels where there is a very narrow focus of programming. Examples of themed channels include:

- The Paramount channel (comedy)
- The Sci Fi channel (science fiction)
- The Discovery channel (factual)
- The History channel (history)
- Bravo (wickedness).

Some of these themes are more sustainable than others, but all owe their success to how well they are promoted and marketed.

In other words to ensuring that people know that when, for example, they tune to Paramount they will get comedy.

Themed channels are an obvious way to wrench audience share from existing operators because:

- They are distinct and different from mass audience channels
- They are an easy way for an audience to find a particular type ('genre') of programming quickly and fast without having to consult a programme guide.

ACCOUNTING GETS IN THE WAY OF THEMING

However, a pure themed channel is hard to create unless (like Paramount) you already own a lot of programme material. For example, if an operator was to set up in competition with Paramount it would need to acquire a vast digital storehouse of comedy material – which would be at a premium price, as sellers would already be aware that there was a demand for pure comedy and raise the price accordingly.

In the real world, themed channel operators have to make do with the ragbags of material which they can pick up from sellers of programme material. Sellers are keen to sell as much programming as possible to buyers regardless of its relevance to the themes pursued by the digital channel owners. This means they often require buyers to take irrelevant material in order to get hold of the material they really want. This was certainly true at the inception of the Sci Fi channel – which aimed to provide viewers with a conduit for pure science fiction programming. Terry Marsh, its first Programme Controller in Europe, recalls that this inadvertently led to the channel's theme being lost behind a whole series of accounting anxieties:

> When you're acquiring you go to Universal or Disney, or someone else, and speak to them about getting some of their product. What they tend to do is throw in other stuff and then charge you slightly more because of it. Now perhaps you didn't want that other stuff – but there are prices allocated against it all. Then the problem begins, because you know that a lot of the stuff you got you don't really want and it actually should be valued at zero and parked. But the finance people, once they

see it, want to 'burn' it – transmit it and use it to fill air time – instead of writing it off on day one and saying 'it was never meant to be'. If you had paid a quarter of a million dollars for a feature film and they had thrown in a series you didn't really want for $60,000, I argued that you should park the series in a very dark vault, give the feature film a value of $310,000, and then amortise the feature film every time that you play it at that value. But the finance people didn't like that. So to a certain extent the channel ended up believing the values of 'science' product from the people who were selling us programmes, and wouldn't allow a re-invention of values on their worth to the channel.

The finance people ended up telling me that I had to schedule that series. So you end up, as Programme Controller, having to muddy the schedule by playing out a series you don't want. In the end I wrote a paper about it all, and I managed to avoid doing it.

We ended up agreeing to re-allocate rights values as soon as a new bundle of programmes comes in. That simplified things a lot. Once you've re-allocated values to something which reflects what the material is worth to you, and as long as it all totals to the value you originally paid for it, you can start playing the material out according to the values of your themed channel.

Compromises were always necessary in the early days at Sci Fi as they didn't have enough material to fully meet their theme aspirations. Terry Marsh got around this by 'stripping programming' – that is, putting out very similar programming at the same times every day. This contrasts with what the old terrestrial networks tend to do – which is to create an 'appointment to view' a particular programme which they had spent a lot of money promoting in order to remind viewers to tune in at a certain time. But that adds costs – it requires a lot of spend for a start-up digital channel to create mass awareness. So Sci Fi was caught between a rock and a hard place – it could not acquire enough relevant material to be 100 per cent 'themed', nor did it have the marketing budget to operate 'appointments to view' successfully.

Where there is a show which creates a certain credibility and starts to get an audience you start to build out on that genre around it, so your viewers get to know there is a block of similar programming there and come back every night. If you go to the major networks, they are retaliating against digital channels by starting to group their programming at certain times of day as well. This is causing hassle from the newspaper critics as they are saying 'yet another night of cookery programmes!' But even the networks can't assume that people will make an 'appointment to view' a particular programme with them any more. Multichannels have forced this change on the networks as their basic tactics have been very sound. They have worked out the sort of person that watches their key programmes and then built on that to give them something they want after those programmes in the schedule.

Although theming is the way to grab audience share off the networks, the process is severely inhibited simply by rights being held in other places. Terry Marsh calculates that it takes three years for a new themed channel to have its maximum impact on a television market, as it takes all that time for the programme rights it desires to come up for renewal. At renewal time a fierce bidding war breaks out, as the themed channel invader comes in to grab rights off the network incumbent. Two things then happen:

- The traditional networks suffer from the loss of some of their stable favourites.
- The price of rights for programming with a specific focus or appeal to a valuable demographic rises. The most obvious examples of this are the battles which break out from country to country for *The Simpsons* as they come up for renewal.

GRABBING A SINGLE BIG HIT

The easiest way to construct a themed channel is to acquire, by hell or high water, a big hit and play it first in a particular territory on your start-up digital channel. This may seem expensive – but it's a lot cheaper than spending all your advertising on building a brand like CBS or ABC.

Channel 4, the UK's 'innovative' channel has, in reality, been making money for years out of being the first choice of the 16–24 year age group. Because this is the group most craved by advertisers, Channel 4 have been able to charge premium advertising rates. But Channel 4 is most worried about incursions into the 16–24 year market by new, well funded broadcasters like MTV, who had a vision of streams of global rock channels aimed specifically at this group.

Channel 4 responded by creating a new digital channel of its own, 'E4'. Its theme is essentially 'entertainment for 16–24 year olds without factual or political content'. That age group seems to reject political and factual content for the moment. But tags like that won't make anyone watch a television channel – so Channel 4 has been forced to acquire something on which to nail the flag of this 'entertainment' theme. It therefore acquired, after a battle royal with Sky One, the UK rights for first runs of *Friends*. It intends to acquire similar programming to put around it on a '*Friends*' theme. Dan Brook, general manager of E4, says he wants 'both old and new episodes of *Friends* to form the core of the channel, around which new programme commissions can be scheduled'.[25]

This demonstrates several interesting lessons about digital channel construction:

- There is no hit like a US hit. Despite all the rhetoric in countries like the UK and France there are no single programmes produced by those countries' creative machines that anyone would risk building a channel around.
- The right single programme will give a feel to a new channel far more powerfully than any kind of advertisement about what the channel is about. As Brook says, 'Sky One has *The Simpsons*, Living has *Jerry Springer*, Paramount has *Frasier*'.

E4 has clearly pursued its agenda of acquiring *Friends* episodes for most of the last year – which reflects Terry Marsh's view that it takes years to acquire the correct rights to get a digital channel on course. *New Media Markets* reports that:

Several options are under consideration for how to use the programme in the schedules, including stripping it across weeknights at the same time, building familiarity. *Friends* on E4 at, for instance, 9 pm would thus become a regular fixture, like *The Simpsons* on Sky One at 7 pm. 'We want to form a regular viewing habit in the schedule' said Brook.

However, the time lag involved in E4's acquisition of the correct programme rights from launch – a year – is not for the faint hearted. First year losses were £38 million. It is unsurprising that the number of digital channels planning to launch in the UK has fallen by a third.

TOTALLY GLOBAL IS TOTALLY OUT OF TOUCH

The importance of US content in building television channels suggests that one day the television world will be ruled unopposed by global digital television channels, all based around US programming. For example, CNN International doesn't attempt to version its US channel for different countries and territories.

However, looking at ratings share in the UK something mysterious separates CNN from Cartoon Network, with a 0.9 per cent share, and from Nickelodeon, which receives a 1.2 per cent share. Both of the latter are global networks. They don't pull ahead of CNN merely because they are aimed at news enthusiasts – they also do something fundamentally different from CNN. Both Nickelodeon and Cartoon network produce a significant amount of local content and splice it in with their network material. Even the mighty MTV, which is a strong contender in the much fought-over 16–24 year old market, has been forced to do the same.

No accountant would recommend this strategy. It involves creating local programmes in all territories in which MTV operates and sending out separate signals to the fifteen countries which receive MTV across Europe. It generates and multiplies costs. But that is precisely what MTV decided to do, led by their Chief Operating Officer in Europe, Simon Guild:

> There were two things going on: one editorial and the other commercial. On the commercial side there was the question of the pan-European advertising market. Now we had a big share of that, because no-one else catered for someone who wanted to run a campaign on a channel which reached all of Europe. There was us and EuroSport and, yes, CNN, but there were few other players.
>
> The big players were ourselves and EuroSport: we probably had 80 per cent of the market, which we still do. But – and this

is a big 'but' – that was less than 1 per cent of the total European advertising market. The rest of advertising spend was taken up with buying space on channels which were simply national, or even smaller.

So commercially, we had to exploit local ad markets to grow the business. However, exploiting a local ad market is very difficult if you're not local. Even if the channel is available it is still hard: buyers just don't buy into it. So that's a driver for being in some way 'local'.

Then simultaneously, from the commercial perspective, we recognised that local editorial decision-making was absolutely critical. How our local channel executives execute language, music, whatever they like – they can position themselves in many different ways, but their decision-making is absolutely key. We started moving towards that, and in '97 we changed the whole thing around completely.

The driving reason for launching MTV's local versions of its channel was therefore simple – advertisers wouldn't buy space on a world channel. Rightly or wrongly, they didn't feel it connected with their target market. As Simon Guild puts it:

> Although we had a local office, our sales marketing office, all the creative and editorial decisions were done in London – the network was coming out of there. It wasn't part of their landscape. Even if we offered the technical possibility of doing it they didn't want to buy, because they felt they weren't connected to it.

So it wasn't just that advertisers wouldn't buy space on a pan-European channel. The problem was that a local German channel originated in London would not attract advertisers either. Advertisers wanted to feel that the channel's content was authentically in touch with its audience, and that meant creating a local editorial staff.

Much is said of the malign effect of advertising pressure on local creativity – but this experience of MTV very much belies that perception.

MTV then undertook one of the most dramatic management transformations in the history of broadcast television. It makes heroic stories from the early days of the terrestrial networks look like a vicarage tea party:

I was a bit extremist about it. I said 'Look, I want everyone to put on a T-shirt on January 1st and it had better have the name of the country on it. If it doesn't have the name of a country on it, you're out of a job'.

We started with a most extreme point of view. The CEO and I decided that the only pan-European people would be him and me. We recognised the fact that some of the value of what we had was that we were a network, and we could operate at a certain scale in some functions.

This was probably the defining moment in the history of this company. We tore up the main Profit and Loss account. We just recreated P&Ls by country, and so we started again from scratch. We realised the business was a hell of a lot better on a regional basis. It was less expensive to run in many respects and much more effective, and much more successful on paper. That was because: (a) commercially we had access to the other 99 per cent of the ad market that we were playing in. Also, suddenly we were accessing a much bigger market from a commercial point of view. And (b) from an editorial point of view you could suddenly grow your ratings in a much more meaningful way and connect to your audience on a local basis, which is really where all the action is.

This strategy would be anathema to many other global channel groups – not only does it appear more expensive at first sight, but also it is much harder to manage. Most broadcasting groups are now very large corporations, like News Corp or Vivendi, who jealously try to centralise and control worldwide operations. Their argument, logically, is that otherwise spending will get out of control and the main brand will get lost in a lot of local misinterpretation.

But MTV believes that its brand is so strong that any local manager can interpret it in his or her own idiom. Simon Guild says a simple message goes out to local MTV managers:

They are in charge. I will not come down and tell them what to do. We want them to be in charge, to take the decisions. We will provide some services from here: some things that are obviously a scale thing. But otherwise there are no givens here. Basically we just task them to grow their businesses. This is what we are tasked to do by the people upstairs. We are a very decentralised organisation. Much more so than any of the other American media companies, where the complete opposite is going on.

We really believe that ultimately it is about trusting your local Manager. The critical decision that you make is deciding who is the Managing Director of your local country. If you hired the right person to run that business you would be just fine. And that's what we focussed on – hiring great people to run our local business.

However, as Simon Guild hints, it takes tremendous nerve for most corporations to adopt this approach. And usually it is only corporations which have deep enough pockets to compete in the television industry.

KELLOGG STRATEGY

A new business strategy which is a notable innovation of MTV's is 'Kellogg strategy'. It is designed to hang onto MTV's market share in territories in which they are facing a lot of competition from music channel rivals – like VIVA in Germany. Music channels have low entry barriers, as they do not have to fight for rights to content in the way in which sports and entertainment channels are forced to do. Pop promoters are happy to give lavish pop videos to channels for free – as long as the channels give the videos airtime. Music channels work on an inversion of the normal television model, in which rights are cheap and so marketing – the only thing which distinguishes them – is all.

Hitting rivals with exemplary marketing is a tiring process – it involves cunning, resource and a constant stream of new ideas. Some of this is dealt with by Simon Guild's critical strategy of devolving management of the channels to the territories at which they are aimed, such as Germany and Italy. With devolved management, the new ideas for marketing the channels will at least originate close to the target audience.

But within those territories there are different demographics for music: for example, audiences for dance music and for 'golden oldies'. To keep rivals out of the music territory MTV creates more and more channels to cater for those audiences, and also 'regionalises' them at the same time. Guild calls it 'Kellogg strategy':

My ultimate model for this was that we would have a channel for every territory. We're going in that direction right now. Today we've got nine or ten MTVs – regional versions of the main MTV channel, which cover the UK, France, Spain, Italy, Germany, Holland, Poland and Scandinavia.

The other thing digital was doing was allowing us to create more channels. Everyone thought 'great, they want more channels'. Towards the end of the '90s we recognised that and there was a strategy which most affected us, the UK, which I call 'Kellogg Strategy'. There are going to be lots of music channels. There are going to be lots of cereals, and you want to have as many as you can. So, like Kellogg's, you want to take up as much of the shelf as you can. So you are looking at Special K and Cornflakes and the rest because clearly you want to be able to offer the consumer maximum choice yourself, rather than create an opportunity for the consumer to go to someone else's channel and deprive you of their eyeballs.

This strategy unmasks a common theme in the development of digital television – conventional business teaching, like cutting back on the variety of products, does not apply.[26] Digital television is a savage fight to increase market share and subscription revenue. Any tactic which achieves that, like an increasing supply of new ideas and channels, is the strategy which any player who can afford it will pursue.

The invasion of Italy

New digital channels have not made great inroads in Italy, essentially because no newcomer is prepared to invest a lot in a small non-English speaking market. RAI and Mediaset (the main state and commercial channels) still cling to 97 per cent of the audience share. Add to that the complication that the owner of Mediaset is also the current Prime Minister, Silvio Berlusconi, and there are formidable barriers to entry. However, the biggest barrier to entry is that which Simon Guild of MTV identified – that it is extremely difficult to make significant inroads into new market if viewers in that market perceive that you are foreign, and so in some way detached from their environment. Sebastiano Musini was a multi-channel pioneer in Italy, setting up MTV there. He saw the problems at first hand:

There is a very well funded and competitive terrestrial market in Italy. Also, whoever was developing alternatives in Italy, like satellite or multichannel platforms, was not Italian. So their programming could not in any way be associated with Italian culture. In the early days of satellite transmission we struggled to find and acquire Italian-originated programming. There were not the production companies. I started with Telepiu in 1996 when there were 80,000 subscribers. When I left in 2000 there were 1 million. So it took four years to get to a million. But when you ask an entrepreneur these are small numbers compared to the numbers of Mediaset and RAI.

So we used a different route with MTV. Italy is unusual in that you can rent space on local terrestrial stations. So that is what we did. In we came with MTV – for six hours on local stations. Then we moved onto one of the national terrestrial frequencies of Telepiu. By 1997 it was 24 hours a day on terrestrial TV. The model was therefore renting out a national frequency – the cost of production was low as it was mainly free music videos, and the demographic was very attractive to advertisers. It's an entity which now makes about 150 billion lira a year in advertising revenues. They reach about half the population, which means about 10 million homes. It was the first thematic channel in Italy. The venture is now owned by SEAT.

But Musini is gloomy about Italian channels taking their place in the elite club of global channels:

I think there are some cultural matrices which work internationally and some of which work locally, as they should. For example, RAI works very well in Italy, and it doesn't work anywhere else. It could be a niche phenomenon linked to those abroad with that sort of cultural matrix. The only successful international cultural matrix which I have seen is that given by those two or three big power-houses with an Anglo-Saxon background: the MTVs, the CNNs. The Coca Colas of television.

However, there are those who think that one sure-fire way to make money out of digital television is to exploit precisely those channels which have a strong specific cultural appeal. This will be dealt with in Chapter 8, *Finding business models that work*.

CHANNEL PRESSURES

The main impact of new digital channels on their environment has been to force existing channels to become much more focused – in effect to produce theming, where a channel is known for a certain limited type of content. This is the only way in which an audience can make quick and easy sense of over 400 channels. However, the rise and rise of theming has brought other pressures to the television market.

Rights

Rights for themes which are thought to deliver a valuable niche audience have shot up in value. Rights to hit shows which appeal strongly to a certain demographic – as *Friends* does to 16–24 year olds – are therefore keenly sought. The old adage in pay television was that there were five strong themes which worked: children's, music, sports, news and movies. But digital is now adding other themes which clearly also can deliver a profit, such as pop music and comedy. The most popular digital channel in the UK is a channel which runs old BBC comedy (and has, as a consequence, an 'old' demographic). Over time, new digital channels will find more niche audiences, and rights will rise in value in other areas of programming.

Conventional networks

Conventional networks have reacted to the attack by the themed channels in two ways:

- Producing themed segments in their schedules
- Creating digital channels of their own which are complementary to the brand of the main channel.

The creation of 'themed' segments has caused critics to accuse the major networks of 'dumbing down', since theming doesn't produce the variety of programming which the main networks used to exhibit. However, in a television market in which the networks are being attacked by highly focused and themed channels, a wide variety of programming is commercial suicide for the networks.

Some networks have created new channels based on their network branding. For example, in the UK Channel 4 has created 'Film Four' and E4 (an entertainment channel). These have cost it £68 million in total and are still not breaking even. Channel 4 claims they have increased its audience share by 30 per cent.[27] But raising the share of the main terrestrial channel from its existing 6 per cent share to an 8 per cent one would have produced the same result. Neither has it helped Channel 4 develop into a global brand: the rights obtained for the new channels tend to be limited to the UK. Grabbing digital market share is a global game – and simply limiting activities to one small market is not a winning strategy. Such myopia has always clouded the vision of the UK networks.

Jim Hytner, Marketing Director of ITV, says that erosion of the audience share of main network channels is now just a fact of life in the digital world, and cannot be countered by creating more and more network branded digital channels:

> Anybody who tells you that share erosion on networks can be made up by the introduction of other channels is talking rubbish. The main benefit of developing other digital channels is not so much in the share but in the relationship with the viewer. You can swap your people from a hit show on a network channel to one on a related digital channel, where they can see an expanded version of the hit show. It not only improves your relationship with your digital viewer, it also improves the relationship for viewers of your main channel.

GLOBAL VISION, LOCAL MANAGEMENT

A critical question for any existing broadcaster should be 'can I make my channel global?' If this is possible (and often it is an expensive 'if') it creates the following competitive advantages:

- Increased audiences
- Increased brand exposure
- Increased opportunities to cross sell other goods or services with the channel brand (consider the revenues which this gives Disney and Nickelodeon)
- Increased advertising revenue and subscriptions.

However, the main obstacles to this strategy are:

- The cost of international programme rights
- The resistance of local audiences to content which does not connect with their culture.

The programme rights issue is easy if you are an MTV – much of your programme material is given to you free of charge. It is also easier if you are a large well-funded terrestrial network (such as Channel 4). Many of the additional costs will be in obtaining world rights to content which is made specially for you. But the real challenge is the tendency of local audiences to reject something which they feel is not made for them – and has no resonance with their culture. MTV has got around this problem by creating regional editorial offices, where staff create strands within a network schedule which address local concerns. Interestingly, without local editorial management advertisers won't buy space either.

This seems to represent a trick which has not occurred to well-funded national broadcasters, who could certainly use the increased audience and revenues that a degree of globalisation brings. An ABC, or a CBS network which has content and strands which is in some part localised for (for example) the French or Italian markets is not beyond the bounds of possibility. What it requires is someone with the vision and commitment to create it.

The Peculiar Rise and Fall of the Platform Owners

WHAT IS A PLATFORM?

Television always sat on something called a 'platform' – but the old platform had two characteristics. It was both ubiquitous and dumb – and therefore no-one was really aware of it. Ubiquity is a positive quality in a platform but dumbness is certainly a very negative quality. Particularly when it comes to making television make money.

A platform is the technology which allows the viewer to receive electronic content. 'Allows' is an important idea in platforms, because a platform is normally the gateway to someone charging you for receiving electronic content. In the UK, where public service broadcasting is funded by a licence fee (a 'television tax'), you are charged according to whether you have any television receivers in your house. The receiver is used as the gateway – without it you cannot receive the pictures. It also leads to the hilarious phenomenon of the licence collection agency touring the UK in 'television detector' vans to see if you have any hidden receivers in your house. Terrestrial broadcasting, where signals radiate from a mast and are picked up by an aerial on your roof, is as much a platform as any of the other systems we are about to examine.

The advantage of the terrestrial broadcasting platform was that it was ubiquitous. For about forty years, it was the only system in town. That meant that it was almost[28] a universal standard. Universal standards are very powerful as they make the technology affordable to viewers and mean that you need little technical expertise to install the receiving equipment. So television, based on a universal standard, spread quickly.

In fact many broadcasters assumed that terrestrial broadcasting, having established a universal standard, was the natural order of things and was a 'natural technological monopoly'. But there is no such thing as a natural technological monopoly, in the sense that one technology becomes so universal that it remains dominant forever. The nature of technology is to produce change and uncertainty – as the story of digital television demonstrates.

Terrestrial television's weakness is that it was dumb. It could not understand who was watching it, or cater for the modern audience or their tastes (as described in Chapter 2). To achieve that required an ability to break out of a restrictive technology, to adopt a technology which would allow a massive number of competing entrants. Only computer technology, with its ability to transmit vast amounts of information using very little bandwidth, could deliver this. This has now made television far more akin to the publishing industry.

This move could not be completed without creating an entirely new platform – a digital television platform. The digital platform is different from the terrestrial system as it involves having a computer in your home to receive and decode the television pictures, which can be sent to your house by satellite, cable, through a mast or through a telephone line. This computer contains software which can be updated by the broadcaster down the link to the computer in the home. The home computer is called a set top box, and produces pictures in a form which a television can understand. It is possible to incorporate the set top box inside the TV – but given the rapid rate of evolution and change in digital television systems this would be a high risk strategy.

Digital television has brought the flexibility of the computer to television – and also its associated uncertainty and pace of change. Everyone in Silicon Valley accepts that their products have about a two-year life cycle (if they are lucky). However, this is an situation which is new and highly disquieting to broadcasting executives. They can cope with *programmes* coming and going – but fundamental change in the way they are sent to the viewer, and the way in which the viewer selects them, requires a level of vision and confidence which many cannot summon.

In moving over to a computer-based technology, several things have happened to television platforms. They have become:

■ *Much more varied:* there are now many systems which allow you to watch television.
■ *Security conscious:* subscription has become an important source of revenue for new television platforms, and platforms have to determine if you are really a subscriber.

- *More able to talk with viewers, and to learn about their tastes:* terrestrial technology had no easy way of doing this.
- *More likely to succeed or fail rapidly.*

It is this last point which seems the most gruesome, particularly for state-licensed broadcasters. Get your platform wrong and you will collapse rapidly – get it right and the next monopoly looks tantalisingly within your grasp.

HOW A DIGITAL PLATFORM IS BUILT

A platform no longer consists of the simple supply line which delivered terrestrial television (see Chapter 1). It has many elements (Figure 4.1). It does this because in order to succeed in digital broadcasting you need many lines of revenue and many reasons for people to return to your platform – regardless of whether or not all those features are money-making or not. Some, like subscriber management, are pure costs – but it is very difficult to run any form of subscription service without subscription management.

A digital platform steers the viewer through a guide which gives them the privilege of accessing certain channels and services, according to how much they are paying in subscription. This leads the viewer to three types of service:

- Television channels
- Interactive services
- Pay per view television.

Pay per view involves the viewer paying extra for special high-value content, like movies, sport or special events. In effect, it accesses a large 'video store' of programmes on demand. Interactivity also allows viewers to buy things, via subscriber management services, over the television. Underpinning all the content on a platform are deals or payments which ensure the platform has the rights to show and sell all its services. It is an electronic market stall. It sells directly to the viewer. Content owners, whether they run channels or just own programmes, sell to it. To the platform owner the struggle is to get good content at a reasonable price. To the content producer the worry is how to get access to the platforms at a reasonable price (as the interview with Peter Bazalgette at the end of this chapter demonstrates).

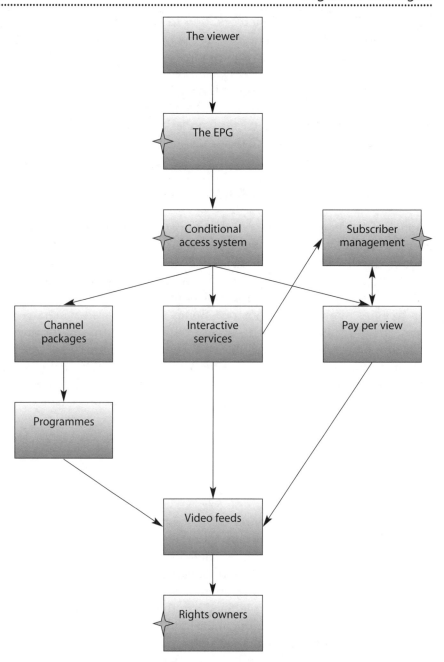

Figure 4.1. The path from viewer to content via the critical elements of a digital television platform

The greatest gains from digital platforms come from their ability to enhance content which is already showing on another part of the platform. For example, Europe was mesmerised in the summer of 2000 by the *Big Brother* format, where 10–12 strangers are trapped in a house for six weeks while television cameras show their attempts to get on with each other – while under the additional pressure of being 'voted out' of the house by a vengeful teenage audience. Transmission space on the main channels is scarce, however – so on an additional digital channel two things happen:

- The television output from the house is shown continuously
- The output of individual cameras can be selected so that you can follow specific individuals on demand using video.

Now this is only possible because the technology allows you both to see channels, use interactive features and see video on demand at will. That is its smartness. However, it also allows the content owner (Endemol) to produce a virtuous circle where you can get its content on demand in any way you want it – and produce an appetite for the main programme on the conventional channel. This is content amplification with a vengeance – increasing its reach, its appeal and its coverage.

Showing its appreciation of the power of content amplification, the UK's Channel 4 has bought the rights to all *Big Brother* formats (including TV, interactive, mobile and merchandising) over the next four years for £40 million.[29]

The *Big Brother* example illustrates the main difference between analogue television and digital: it fundamentally changes the relationship with the audience. On digital television the audience can demand content, purchase content, and can even create personal selections of programming. It is the difference between the tendency of analogue to ration content and the tendency of digital to create a content supermarket. The supermarket can even keep a record of viewers' 'till receipts', and advertise content to them which it knows to be of interest.

There are four main elements which are essential to this closer relationship with the viewer (on the figure they have acquired a star to show their importance):

- The EPG, or electronic programming guide
- The conditional access system

■ The subscriber management centre
■ Rights acquisition and content deals for the platform.

The electronic programme guide

The electronic programme guide is something that a digital system needs simply because of the amount of content available. It allows viewers to navigate the content and make sense of it. The simplest are based on a time-line schedule which allows the viewer to select a channel – the television then switches to the output of that channel.

Some EPGs allow you to see as much as seven days ahead. This is because it allows for the addition of a personal planner – the viewer can pre-select programmes which he or she would like to see, and is then reminded of them as they are about to start.

The electronic programme guide is, in a sense, an active advertising hoarding, as it gives prominence to programmes or content that you might otherwise ignore. It is also the first thing which the viewer encounters when they decide to sample new content. The owner of the platform is the ultimate controller of this gateway, which is why EPGs assume such importance. Negotiations about who will occupy the first five places on the EPG are often tortuous and hard-fought. They are also a contest between the platform owner's need for content and the platform owner's need to get prominence for the channels they own.

Interactivity is also reached via the gateway. However, some interactivity is achieved by pressing a button while a programme is playing. For example, different camera angles on a football match are reached from the main game. In this way, content owners try to harness the powers of 'content amplification' which digital platforms provide.

Some systems[30] have moved rapidly towards quite complex search EPGs – which allow you to search a system by selecting the details of a particular actor or director and see which films of their films are playing on the platform. This kind of search is invaluable as it allows smart platforms to gather data on viewers' preferences.

The conditional access system

The conditional access system is strategically the most important piece of software in a digital television platform. It decides if it will let you onto the system, and what it will let you see. It checks your privileges by reading the card information (if the platform uses credit card type verification) or takes information direct from a subscriber database (more typical on cable systems).

Conditional access systems for digital platforms are highly specialised. Rupert Murdoch's News Corp based the BSkyB system on a conditional access system designed by Professor Adi Shamir at the Weizman Institute of Science in Jerusalem. Prof. Shamir is one of the world's experts on encryption. Murdoch liked it so much he bought 80 per cent of Shamir's company.

The conditional access system has to be secure – if it can be broken, it allows viewers in without paying a subscription. A platform with many freeloading subscribers haemorrhages both reputation and cash. Canal Plus, the European television platform owned by Vivendi, has had huge security problems. It is estimated that 33 per cent of Canal Plus viewers in Italy and Spain access it illegally. Canal Plus has recently brought a legal suit against Murdoch's NDS operation alleging that they broke the Canal Plus code and helpfully published it on hackers' websites. NDS deny this and say that the Canal Plus conditional access system was fundamentally insecure from day one – an accident waiting to happen.

The conditional access system talks to, and is controlled by, the subscription management centre. Changing the package to which you subscribe means the centre will tell the conditional access software to let you onto a different range of services, or withdraw them altogether if you don't pay your bills.

The subscriber management centre

Call centres were the growth industry of the 1990s. A digital platform's subscription management centre is yet another variety of call centre. It deals with calls from subscribers asking about:

- Taking out new subscriptions (and arranging equipment installation)
- Changing the channels and services to which the viewer has subscribed
- Technical problems and enquiries.

This is mundane stuff, but get it wrong and the platform suffers. BSkyB spent an entire year improving subscriber management handling as part of their campaign to reduce the rate of churn of their service (people cancelling after a year of trying it out). But it is very labour intensive. The collapse of ITV Digital in the UK, which only had 1.2 million subscribers, led to the loss of 1,500 jobs at call centres in Wales, Devon and London. That implies a ratio of one subscriber manager to every 1,000 subscribers.

Rights acquisition and content deals

Getting content which will attract and hold subscribers is the primary critical success factor for the management of a digital platform. It is all about getting to content before someone else spots its potential, and then tying up the rights exclusively (if this is possible). In fact digital platforms would not have got off the ground had the old terrestrial broadcasters not realised a number of truths:

- That they were undercharging for certain types of content (like football and films)
- That there was a much bigger appetite for many more forms of content than they were providing
- That television combines well with certain features of digital platforms (like the ability to order content or to interact with the outcome of television programmes).

However there is a dilemma for platform owners in that certain content owners will only join the platform if the price is right. That often means that much of the platform's valuable subscription revenue is swallowed up by sharing it with channels and content providers which a platform feels it needs.

For example, BSkyB gives in excess of £1.00 for every subscriber receiving the Disney channels via its platform. However, go to BSkyB and offer them a new business channel and they are unlikely to offer any cut of the subscription revenues at all. That is because BSkyB feels that it is much more powerful, given its audience profile, to have Disney content than to have yet more business channels. It believes Disney Channels will deliver subscribers.

So running a platform is rather like running a football or baseball team – you need star players, but you often also have to pay top dollar for them. Creating a successful platform involves a series of very fine deals and judgements.

TYPES OF DIGITAL PLATFORM

There are four basic types of digital platform:

- *Satellite:* like DirecTV in the US or BSkyB in the UK
- *Terrestrial:* like ITV Digital in the UK or Quiero TV in Spain (both now defunct)
- *Cable:* like NTL or UPC in Europe
- *Broadband:* a new flavour of digital TV delivered over the Internet.

Small stations fight the spread of digital in the US

The spread of digital transmission in the USA has been slow. For now, it is offered by DirecTV (satellite) or over cable in the big cities. About 70 per cent of US commercial television stations will miss a government deadline in May 2002 to upgrade their equipment in preparation for digital transmission. The slow spread of digital in the USA has been attributed to the lack of set top boxes and also to the economics of US TV – where there are lots of small television stations that don't want to invest a lot for returns which will be absorbed mainly by the content owners. 'There are no benefits and a lot of costs' said Del Parks, Vice President for Sinclair Broadcasting Group Inc. of Baltimore. However, were these stations not to upgrade they would be at a distinct disadvantage against digital satellite competitors like DirecTV, as experience in Europe has shown.[31]

All of these require different paths to deliver digital signals into the home. This gives them all different strengths and weaknesses.

Satellite

This has the most universal coverage. It is possible to get a strong satellite signal to a wide area, spanning several countries. The signal is received through a small dish on the house. The only things which impede the signal are buildings and trees. In northern countries, such as the USA and most of Europe, the dish has to point almost horizontally at the satellite, which is on the horizon. This makes buildings and trees an issue in some areas.

Satellite's weakness is that it has to beg, steal or borrow a return line from a telecommunications company. The return line allows the subscriber to communicate directly with the subscriber centre and order movies and goods through the television. In the UK BSkyB is forced to use a British Telecom line, and sees none of the revenue generated by communication between the set top box and the subscriber centre. Cable has the advantage that it pockets this revenue.

Terrestrial

This should be the easiest way to receive digital signals, as it merely involves plugging a box into your existing aerial connection. In reality it is beset by weaknesses. These are (in no particular order):

- The need to squeeze digital signals onto the same terrestrial frequencies as the analogue signals means that terrestrial digital has a significantly lower carrying capacity than satellite. It can only manage a maximum of about sixty channels. Most countries which offer terrestrial promise that when the analogue frequencies are turned off some will be made available to digital terrestrial. But don't hold your breath.
- The signals are weak. If they were stronger they would interfere (in Europe) with those of foreign broadcasters. In the UK, this has meant that coverage has been far from universal.

Both of these weaknesses were part of a potent cocktail of business errors which have already forced the digital terrestrial platforms of the UK and Spain to close (see 'What Can Go Wrong?' later in this section). Sweden's is also struggling.

Cable

Technically a very good way of supplying digital pictures into the home, as it allows almost infinite channel capacity and also a big return line. This has allowed it to pioneer video on demand (that is, video which plays to your TV as and when you want it).

Cable also has an existing revenue model as it can practice what is known as 'triple play' – that is, its subscribers pay revenues for telephony, television channels and Internet connection. (Kingston Communications in the UK has also claimed to have found a fourth – e-commerce conducted over the television – but this is slightly stretching a point.) This normally means that cable can achieve a very high Average Revenue Per User – the holy grail of platforms in periods of low subscriber growth.

However, the two main weaknesses of cable mean that cable companies have an almost inbred tendency to consolidate. The weaknesses are:

- The right to cable a neighbourhood, although a monopoly, is awarded in small parcels. That means that in order to create a nationwide cable broadcasting system you have to either acquire or merge with other franchises. This has meant running up big debts to pay for the acquisitions. Though rival cable systems seem compatible often their technology is not, and a lot of work has to be put into achieving economies of scale from the merger of several cable operations.

- It is expensive to install. You have to dig up the streets to get to people's homes and that means spending lots of capital. That has meant that whatever the cash flowing in from telephony, television and data they have rarely been large enough to make a profit after taking debt repayments into account. Such a fate has befallen AT & T's cable operations in the USA (which are currently up for sale). A graphic example is Telewest in the UK – Telewest still needs to spend £500 million in 2002 to introduce video on demand, and its interest payments on its £5 billion debt are almost as large. But the company only generates £400 million in cash a year. Why did the cable companies get their sums so wrong? They simply believed their own rhetoric and grossly over-stated their own projections. But then everyone was doing the same. After an even bigger series of imbalances and misjudgements, Europe's UPC cable network was snapped up at a knockdown price by John Malone's Liberty Media of the USA.

Down the tubes

Cable has had a rocky ride. United Pan-Europe Communications (UPC), the Dutch high-speed cable group, has enjoyed a history marked by far-sighted vision and disaster. It sold the market a very ambitious business plan based on providing the digital 'triple play' of telephony, Internet and television services – but messed it up and got found out.

UPC is potentially available to 7.1 million cable customers – but they are simply receiving basic multichannel television. Their digital set top box attracted only 50,000 subscribers in a year. Some of the problem was down to Microsoft software, which had to be dumped. It was yet another example of Microsoft proving singularly unsuccessful at penetrating the mainstream television market.

This left UPC with a funding gap (in other words, the money it would need to pay its way before breaking even) of about 1 billion Euro. In the end Liberty Media, John Malone's USA based investment company, turned a $896 million loan into a 76 per cent equity stake in the company. Rivals and admirers viewed this as yet another example of Malone picking up an ailing (or failing) digital broadcasting company with great assets on the cheap. This gives Malone 7.1 million cable subscribers concentrated in the Netherlands, Austria and the Nordic region.

One of the most disappointing failures for broadband enthusiasts was that of Excite @home in the States. Born as the result of a $6.7 billion merger between Excite, the portal and @home, the broadband access business, the idea was that broadband would be the growing area of connectivity, and would be irresistible if coupled with content from Excite.

Excite @home managed to land exclusive deals to supply broadband services to three of the major US cable companies: AT & T, Comcast and Cox. But the deal was flawed, as under its terms 65 per cent of broadband subscriber fees went to the three cable companies. Excite then proceeded to go madder than most in the dot com boom by purchasing an online greeting cards company called Bluemountain.com for $780 million. Its founders headed for the blue hills with the loot, while the acquisition failed to live up to its promise and was later sold for $35 million. The Vice President of Strategy at Cox, Dallas Clement, wryly commented, 'The company lost track of the importance of broadband customers'.

Service deteriorated in the core broadband business and Excite had to take a write-down of $4.6 billion. It went into liquidation and its exclusive cable partners went their own way, one of them (AT&T) losing a $4 billion investment. A million broadband users lost their service provider.

However, over 85 per cent of US homes potentially have access to broadband – so it looks as though it is the great Trojan horse outside the citadel of the television operators, despite its shaky start.

Broadband

Broadband Internet access is in its infancy but poses an interesting threat to the world of existing (and consolidating) conventional platforms. This is due to the power and determination of the set top box manufacturers, particularly in the USA. Broadband is a broad enough Internet connection to bring full-screen television pictures straight into the home via the telephone line. It operates at a stream rate of about 500kb/sec, as opposed to the 56kb/sec rate used by conventional dial-up home modems. The spread of broadband is well advanced in the USA and in Germany. At the moment 11.6 per cent of US households have broadband access. Merrill Lynch estimates that this will increase to 50 per cent by 2008. This would make it a very viable alternative means of television delivery into the home.[32]

This is, of course, an alternative means of television distribution. Attach a clever box to a broadband line and it is possible to circumvent the paraphernalia of cables, satellites and masts which make up conventional television distribution. With the right agreements with the telecom network operators in place, it is possible – in theory – to create your own global television networks. With the vast overcapacity on the world's global networks, the creation of private television networks is beginning to make perfect economic sense.

Personal computers aren't optimised to act as television decoders – so the missing link in this broadband vision is the set top box. Most set top box technology is given away free – and the costs recouped eventually through subscriptions. That means that set top box technology tends to be cheap and have low functionality, just to keep costs down.

Broadband Internet access can be delivered both over cable and over high-speed telephone lines (known as Digital Subscriber Lines, or DSL). Telecoms consultancy BWCS estimates that DSL will be more popular in Europe than in the US in five years time –

but that the US will retain its broadband lead when other platforms, like cable, are taken into consideration.[33]

People like Paul Allen (co-founder of Microsoft with Bill Gates) have leapt into this vacuum and are investing millions in set top boxes which track your preferences as you watch and record (to hard disc) programmes in which you might be interested. The boxes also supply the latest games and games platforms. In effect, the boxes are infinitely changeable platforms which can offer state of the art functionality. They ought to be. Paul Allen's box, Moxi, which won best-of-show at the consumer electronic festival in Las Vegas in January 2002 has so far consumed $67 million in development – and is still eating money.

Niche broadcasting using DSL

Interesting niche opportunities are opening up as a result of broadband distribution. The BBC acquired a play out centre and network for video distribution via broadband from Intel Corporation, who had decided it was not a core element of their activities. When they examined their gift horse, the BBC discovered that the Intel network had superb broadband connections into North America. An early customer was Sky Sport, who had discovered that expatriate Indians in California would pay about $100 to see a complete cricket test match delivered via broadband direct to their computer (the technology involved in doing this is described in the set top box section). Sky has the rights, so they used the play out centre to distribute cricket via Internet connections direct to computers in California. This obeys the first law of the Internet – it is a great way to serve a market which is both niche and global. Interestingly Richard Brooke comments in Chapter 8 that one of the few unambiguously profitable business models in digital television is foreign content for expatriate ethnic groups.

But the threat is serious. Digital television has so far demonstrated its ability to change the settled television equation so fast and so often that only the best managements will survive the process. And the television industry doesn't have many tried and tested managements – as they have been used to too predictable an environment for too long. That is a big opportunity for anyone with vision, funding and experience of how to generate revenues. Broadband offers a means of entry to such entrepreneurs.

WHAT CAN GO WRONG?

In the early days of platforms, their potential seemed infinite. It quickly became clear that viewers were prepared to pay subscriptions directly to see material which they couldn't get easily (or conveniently) on traditional free to air channels. In fact subscription rates have turned out to be in the range of $30–$100/month. With 39 per cent of UK households subscribing to digital television systems, and 15 million households subscribing to Canal Plus in Europe, what could possibly go wrong?

Unless platform operators steer their businesses with the delicacy of a bomb disposal expert removing a detonator the answer is 'everything'. There have been three very public digital television platform collapses so far, all of them in Europe:

- *ITV Digital*, the terrestrial digital platform, which collapsed in April 2002 having burnt £1 billion of investors' money.
- *Quiero TV*, Spain's digital terrestrial platform, which closed at the point at which it was losing 24 million Euro/month.
- *Premier*, Kirch Media's Pay TV platform in Germany (which is satellite based) has gone into insolvency with losses of 3.2 billion Euro.

A fourth collapse seems not far off. Senda, Sweden's troubled digital terrestrial operator, has so far attracted only 100,000 subscribers since its launch in April 2000.[34]

The highest-profile of these disasters is ITV Digital, which crashed and burned after it found it had no prospect of breaking even (although at that time it had 1.2 million subscribers). At the heart of ITV Digital's demise was paying too much for content, in particular minor league football for which it paid £315 million for three years – a price peak which will never be seen again. However, it was also beset by a whole string of subsidiary business problems which can only be put down to management incompetence:

- It came to market *third* behind already established cable and satellite platforms – something that any marketing advisor will tell you never to do. The problem is that as third to market you will be forced to play catch-up: you will be compared with the stronger propositions in the market, and finally the whole development of the market will be dictated by the stronger players. This is exactly what happened, with ITV Digital desperate to rival BSkyB by running a poor imitation of it.

- It had inferior technology: the signal was not strong enough to give the platform universal coverage, nor was the system's capacity great enough to rival the offerings of satellite and cable. It then tried to market this inferiority using the slogan 'managed choice' (*i.e.* a choice so narrow you can understand what it is). This belittled the intelligence of the consumer – a very dangerous strategy.

- It always had problems with its conditional access software (see box earlier in the chapter). This meant that many of its subscribers were getting it free. If word gets around that free content is available, this spells death to subscription services.

Its management have argued that the technology problems were not of their own making – but the fact is that in digital television management must have a combination of both technology and business experience. Otherwise they cannot assess risks and opportunities in the digital television market. This is a lesson which is little understood – particularly when broadcasting executives stray into areas in which they have no competence. Unfortunately, for most, that area now includes the future of their industry.

Why did ITV Digital's management embody such ignorance and take such stupendous risks? Rupert Murdoch commented on this intriguing question when he reacted to the ITV Digital fiasco by saying:

ITV Digital did not have to pay anything like £315 million to get the football rights, which were available for much less. But the story of ITV digital is a story of incompetence from day one. The truth is that the ITV monopolists who have been spoon-fed for more than thirty years have shown themselves incapable of doing anything very well except sucking up to regulators. Everything has been given them [by the regulators] and they screwed everything up. The result is that the UK does not have a decent privately owned TV company except BSkyB which had to go outside the system.'[35]

Prebble makes waves

Stuart Prebble had the dubious privilege of being brought into ITV Digital as a CEO with a 'safe pair of hands' after the removal of its first CEO, Stephen Grabiner. Prebble made a series of very open comments about ITV Digital at a dinner the day before the administrators finally decided to pull the plug on it. Prebble's list of reasons for the platform's failure make interesting reading, if only because of their disproportionate emphasis on the competition it faced, the regulators and its shareholders' lack of guts. The last resort of a failing 'safe pair of hands'? Very possibly – but you have to see it from Prebble's point of view.

- He accused BSkyB of an 'aggressive' stance towards the platform after BSkyB was forced to leave the original digital terrestrial consortium, because the competition authorities had insisted its presence was monopolistic.
- Prebble said that 'the simple fact is that we do not have a regulatory environment in this country geared up to dealing with a ruthless and determined abuser of dominance. Sky's mixture of aggression and intimidation, exercised through its legal and regulatory team and the political power that comes from its media empire, has effectively neutered any of the systems which could and should have prevented them from eliminating competition from this market place'.
- Prebble admitted that problems with reception and power had cost ITV Digital 750,000 subscribers.
- He also said that ITV Digital's business plan did not allow for the free distribution of set top boxes – a move forced on it when BSkyB distributed set boxes free. He omitted to say that because BSkyB was a member of the original digital terrestrial consortium they knew the effect free boxes would have on ITV Digital's business plan.

Prebble finally admitted that management made mistakes. 'Do I blame ourselves? Absolutely. We seriously underestimated the resource and determination of the competition, and we even more seriously overestimated the resilience and determination of the competition authorities. We made mistakes in our content proposition. We took on Rupert Murdoch without the depth of resources and strength of nerve to see it through. We had technical problems and we failed to solve them.'

In the end, ITV Digital had made so many mistakes it wasn't safe even in the safest of hands.

WHAT CAN GO RIGHT?

The truth is that the probability of making a new television platform a success is very small. The only operators to have achieved
this unambiguously so far in Europe are Murdoch's BSkyB and
Vivendi's Canal Plus. But only one of these (BSkyB) is making a
profit. Canal Plus made losses of $336 million in 2001, but has
15.6 million subscribers in eleven countries throughout Europe.
With that many subscribers the operation is worth a fortune,
despite the problems of its parent Vivendi. BSkyB has 5.4 million
subscribers in the UK. Running since the early nineties, when it
was struggling for finance it is now worth £14.5 billion – which is
more than the value of its 40 per cent owner News Corp.

So what did BSkyB, the only profitable platform in Europe, get
right? The list is simple. It had to:

- Get the right content
- Make sure that the best bits of that content are exclusive to
  your platform
- Get that content at the right price
- Make sure that there is so much content that no one else can
  easily compete
- Obtain conditional access technology which is secure
- Create a subscriber management service which ensures that
  customers enjoy uninterrupted viewing
- Ensure that the service is inexpensive to buy and easy to install
- Ensure that the service can be universally received
- Ensure that the service is future proof, to the extent that it can
  combine several media to produce 'content amplification' and
  rising revenue per subscriber.

Reducing the list just to two imperatives: the secret of success is
to get the *right technology* running the *right content*. Most commen-
tators believe that the technology can be sorted easily. However the
experiences of Canal Plus (and then ITV Digital) suggest that this
is easier said than done. Canal Plus estimates that losses from the
hacking of its conditional access software stand at $1 billion. In
Italy, cable installers now offer pirated Canal Plus cards at a
discount – and these cards now account for a third of Italian viewers.[36] Instead of paying a regular subscription, purchasers make a
one-off payment of $100 and get the whole package.

Just as important is getting the right content at the right price. A large factor in Canal Plus's losses is the exorbitant amounts they paid for the rights to football and to Formula One racing.

Matthew Symonds of *The Economist* sees this as the main stumbling block to making a success of a platform, and believes that the fierce competition for rights has significantly dented BSkyB's profits:

> You're always in a little bit of dilemma, because on the one hand you want to attract as many people as possible to the platform: that means that the content on the platform has to be as comprehensive and as attractive as possible. On the other hand, you want to make sure that the channels that you are carrying are not getting too rich off you. BSkyB makes a brilliant job of that.
>
> Sky was very profitable and is no longer very profitable. There are two reasons why it has ceased to be profitable. One was the migration to digital, in which they believed they had to drive that migration as fast as possible in order to stop other platforms from gaining advantage over them. Basically, they felt that they had to bring the advantage that they had in the analogue world into the digital world while they had the option to do so, and that meant *giving away set top boxes*.
>
> The other reason they lost their profitability was that they used Premier League football from the beginning to drive uptake of the platform. They got it extremely cheaply first time round. The second time they paid, I would say, the full economic price. The third deal, which is coming into operation now, I think they've overpaid for. I don't think they will get their money back on it. I would agree with Greg Dyke that Premier League rights, and sports rights generally, have for a time reached a peak.
>
> Sky had a problem that if they didn't come up with enough money the Premier League had a plan of its own to create its own football channel and contract out the running of it to a broadcaster. If you are in a defensive position, when Sky were trying to grow the platforms as fast as possible they could not afford to be underbid. But the money they were able to make off the back of the first deal was a hell of a lot more than they were paying to the Premier League. Flip-flop the other way round now. The money passes through from Sky to the players, barely passing the clubs as it goes.

The CEO of BSkyB, Tony Ball, is now talking to analysts about not bidding for some sports rights, and also about dropping the output of one Hollywood studio. He is more relaxed now that ITV Digital is gone – and it is also a good negotiating position to start from when renewing rights. Eager analysts immediately marked up BSkyB shares.

BSkyB created the model for how content is paid for by a platform. They created two categories of content: the 'crown jewels' (things which people would probably subscribe to the platform to see) and the 'ought to haves' – things which would keep people watching.

For the crown jewels they paid money up front in expensive fixed-price deals. These deals were negotiated exclusively to the platform, and included rights to the Premier League (the top football league) and the movie output of several Hollywood studios. For the 'ought-to-haves' BSkyB gave channel owners (such as Disney and Nickelodeon) a share of the subscription income. This is a very delicate game, as there is a danger that 'ought-to-haves' will walk off with income which ideally would come to the platform. The way to play it successfully is to have a clear idea of the channels you don't want and offer them no subscription income. Most of the channels which fail on BSkyB are in this latter category – but the platform is obliged by the UK regulator to take any channel which wishes to have carriage. Their problem, without subscription income, is that most are economically unviable unless they have a very original business model (see Chapter 8).

The other element which must be got right is the delivery system. The part which resides in the consumer's home is called the set top box. The dilemma for digital platform owners is how much intelligence and memory to put in the box. The more you invest in it, the more expensive it gets. This wouldn't matter except that in the UK consumers have got used to receiving the box free at the point of delivery. In Germany, where Kirch Media charged for set top boxes, the platform went into administration. So far only in the US has it been viable to charge for set top boxes for digital platforms.

As it is, set top box design and delivery look as though they will continue to form the technological battleground over which the future of digital television is fought. Much of that battle will be about standards.

NOTHING IS STANDARD

In the world of analogue television, sound and pictures came to an aerial on a house's rooftop, and pulsed and flexed the electromagnetic spectrum in sympathy with the television pictures. The transmissions occupied a motorway-full of electromagnetic spectrum (see Chapter 1).

Digital distribution, however, involves turning television pictures into computer code. This has the advantage that the picture, in getting to the house, occupies far less bandwidth. But all digital systems are only viable if there are universal encoding (and decoding) standards for television pictures. So far, two types of television encoding have emerged and are widely used:

- The MPEG family
- Streaming media.

MPEG

The Motion Picture Experts Group works with the International Standards Organisation to come up with standards for encoding video and audio data. There are currently five MPEG standards: MPEG 1, MPEG 2, MPEG 4, MPEG 7 and MPEG 21. Most current digital television systems distribute MPEG 2. This allows television pictures to be sent to the set at a rate of 2 megabits/second. On cable, terrestrial and satellite systems there is enough bandwidth to transmit at this rate. MPEG 4 is a new standard in which the pictures are even more highly compressed, and so less bandwidth is required. It also allows content to sit on many different devices (such as mobile 3G phones and 'hand-held personal assistants').

Streaming media

Streaming media is an entirely separate video standard which has been evolved for the Internet and the personal computer. It has a strange characteristic – when it is played it can't be recorded. This is because it is like a stream of water which empties into a 'bucket' on the computer. Only when there is enough data in the bucket will it give you pictures and sound. As the pictures play the bucket empties, to be filled by more of the data stream.

The advantage of streaming is that it will work at very low data speeds. It is possible to get sound and vision for a quarter-frame picture on a PC with just 40 kb/sec (2 per cent of the capacity of the MPEG 2 standard). The low data rate is achieved by electronic sleight of hand: the data is compressed by removing features, colour and definition so that it can be sent on a very low band stream. The 'bucket' mechanism is simply to get over the tendency of bit rates on the Internet to jump up and down continually. A picture needs a consistent stream – which is what the bucket provides. The data disappears after playing to ensure that a predilection to watch video on your PC doesn't give your hard disc constipation.

Why worry about a nerdy standard for people using PCs – when television has MPEG? The answer is because the latest streaming players (the software which enables you to look at a stream) are getting so good that they can give you VHS-quality full screen pictures – particularly when the bit rate into the computer is of a broadband standard (500kb/sec). There is no reason on earth why digital television providers shouldn't use a streaming standard, if it is good enough. There are three popular streaming standards:

- *Windows Media Player* (backed by Microsoft): now present on all new Microsoft Internet browsers (which makes it ubiquitous).
- *Real Player* (from RealNetworks): Real claim that their software is on 92 per cent of the world's PCs – a claim which is fiercely disputed by Microsoft.
- *Quicktime*: an old standard from Apple which has failed to achieve lift-off.

Windows and RealNetworks have very different business models. Microsoft bundles up its Windows Media Player in the software you get with a new PC at no extra cost. It is also free to download off the Internet. Real sells you a RealOne for $9.95 monthly subscription which includes a bundle of content. Content includes Music-Net, a joint venture between Real and three major record labels. There are also video content deals with ABC News, Sports.com, the NBA and the Wall Street Journal.

The interesting aspect of RealNetworks' business model is that it is essentially a digital content service aimed primarily at the spread of broadband out across the US and Europe. It is a direct challenge to digital television platforms, in fact.

The set top box

At its heart, the set top box is a small computer which decodes the television signals coming into it from satellite, cable or terrestrial transmission. But there's more to it than that.

The gateway into the box goes via the conditional access system, which is the security software which determines which channels and content you are allowed to see. The settings of the conditional access system can be altered by the subscription management centre, which keeps a database of individual customers. There are very distinct encryption and conditional access systems – for example, Canal Plus Technologies conditional access system is called Mediaguard and BSkyB's is called Videoguard. However there are other conditional access systems – supplied by Liberate and OpenTV in the US.

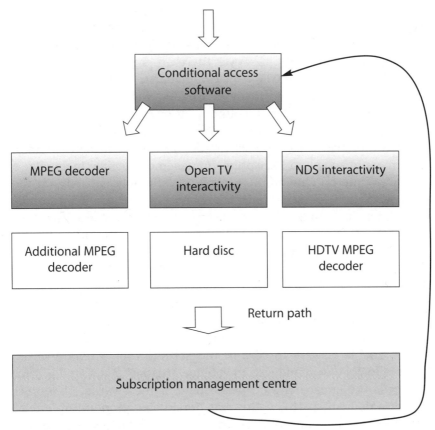

Figure 4.2. The essential components of set top box architecture

The conditional access software is linked with that of the Electronic Programme Guide which tells viewers what is scheduled to run on the channels. In some systems (like Sky's) this does not tell you about 'video on demand' that is available on the system – which in Sky's case can only be accessed via a channel. The interactive software which enables most of Sky's video on demand clips (such as its excellent interactive news system) was also supplied by NDS. It relies on clips which are held temporarily in the box memory. Consequently, on-demand video clips can't be very long.

Electronic programme guides on some systems are much more sophisticated. For example, Kingston Communications' DSL-based system allows viewers to search by favourite directors or actors for programmes they want to see. It is much closer to a 'Google' search on the Internet than leafing through a listings magazine.

BSkyB's boxes, like TPS's boxes in France, have OpenTV software on them which allows viewers to browse, play games and buy over the television. OpenTV doesn't allow viewers onto the Internet, as it works on a 'walled garden' principle (in other words, a web which is closed off from the web). However there are systems that do allow viewers onto the web via TV – for example, the MHEG-5 interactive television standard. This involves turning web pages (which are high-resolution) into lower resolution TV pages. TV screens are not made up of such a dense forest of lines as PC screens.

Any interactive use of the set top box means using some kind of 'return path' to the subscription management centre (normally a telephone line on satellite). On cable, it is simply capacity on the cable system. The return path often has to be secure (for example when a transaction is taking place over it), and there are also standards for this. BSkyB uses an authentication process called 'SSSL'.[37] This enables companies offering interactive services over the Sky platform to check creditworthiness and collect card payments. Sky demands a fixed payment for the use of this service and then 5 per cent of revenues after that. Cable competitors plan to use a rival system, the Liberate DTV Navigator 1.2 technology.

MTV has recently started using the return line out of the set top box to enable viewers to vote in the MTV Europe Music Awards. Viewers to MTV were allowed to vote for artists they wanted to win, to access the latest news on performers at the awards, or to take part in a daily quiz. This voting was done using premium rate telephone calls – 25 pence for each vote cast and 50 pence to enter the quiz. These revenues were all split between BSkyB, MTV and the telephone company.[38] MTV believes the technology creates a close emotional link between the viewer and the event. They have encouraged viewers watching *Videoclash* to send in SMS text messages from their mobiles to vote for their preferred music video.

To a certain extent the functionality of the set top box can be upgraded. This is done overnight by a software download, either through the satellite or the cable. The problem with downloads is that set top boxes, like computers, often need re-booting when they are over. This has to be done by the user. BSkyB has recently added a 'personal planner' which alerts you when a programme you have bookmarked is about to start using an upgrade.

Keeping prices down has limited the set top box architecture in Europe to the basic features described so far. However in the US – where there is a culture of getting the consumer to pay for the box – there are, unsurprisingly, a large variety of features on offer. For example DirecTV offers a number of boxes with its satellite system – which shoots pictures and services at the US from four mighty Hughes-built satellites:

- *Multichannel receiver:* capable of receiving all the digital channels listed in Appendix A of this book.
- *HDTV receiver:* a box capable of receiving high-definition pictures. HDTV supplies so many lines on a screen that it is possible to watch a football game on a single wide shot (as you can still see the ball). HDTV didn't really take off in Europe as platform owners thought that many channels with low definition would be more appealing than a few with HDTV. But in the US you can have it all.
- *Interactive set top box:* with the interactive features which are incorporated as standard into European set top boxes. DirecTV were never so convinced that viewers would try to buy things over the TV programme controller, so interactivity is optional.
- *Ultimate TV:* a Microsoft box which lets you record and retrieve two programmes simultaneously on a hard disc. As the box records programmes automatically, you can retrieve shows you missed using a search facility. It also has access to the web and e-mail.
- *TiVo receiver:* TiVo also features automatic hard disc recording with two tuners. On TiVo the box can be programmed to search out and record your favourite shows, and also programmes made by your favourite actors and directors.

BSkyB now also offers Sky Plus – which has some TiVo-like features. They charge a flat amount plus a £10/month subscription – very similar to the DirecTV pricing model. It is claimed that households that have TiVo only watch 30 per cent of their programming from conventional channels. The rest is all taken from recordings to the hard disc. As there is no quality loss involved in watching a digital programme recorded to a hard disc, it would be hard for the viewer to tell (or care about) the source of the programmes.

The Europeans have taken fewer risks with their set top boxes – favouring a fixed offering over an infinite variety with many different price points. It is cheaper to run a business with fewer products as long as you are sure they will sell. However, the appetite for personal video recorders (the generic term for TiVos and Ultimate TV) is likely to make a limited set top box offering a thing of the past.

THE FUTURE OF THE SET TOP BOX

An interesting statistic from US brokerage Robertson Stephens indicates that set top box technology from Canal Plus, BSkyB and DirecTV now reaches 80 million subscribers worldwide. It goes on to estimate that this should grow to 210 million by 2005.[39] However, it is not clear that we will be using set top boxes in their present form in five years, and even less in ten years, from now. The only constant of digital television is its predisposition for turning existing business models on their head.

Developments in Japan suggest that digital television is moving on rapidly again. Sony President Kunitake Ando says, 'We think consumers will use their TVs like a server to download and manage most of their entertainment audio and video content, because TVs will always serve the captive audience'.

President Ando has put his finger on the most attractive feature of the television audience – their need to sit and relax. This makes them far more likely to take to entertainment on demand. However, it is small step from using a digital set top box to do that to using your own storage system to do it. After all, with the set top box all you are doing is using a remote storage system which is managed by someone else. Why not use your own?

Sony has developed a prototype product called the Personal Network Home Storage System, which can store 450 hours of DVD content, the content of 1,500 CDs and 600,000 high-resolution images. Using a home network which uses wireless connections, consumers will be able to use the TV to manage and interact with their Walkmans, Playstations and video cameras.[40] Steve Jobs of Apple is thinking the same way. He sees the home computer becoming the centre of a home network from which all audio and video entertainment is drawn.

If all this activity by both Sony and Apple seems in large part self-serving – it is. But there is a logic to the argument that entertainment content should be ordered and stored by the home user. All that is happening is that the content store is moving out of the hands of the media moguls and into the home. That is the same as has happened with arranging programmes as channels, as schedules and scheduling are being ignored. And it is certainly the model for publishing where books are kept on shelves in the home – and 'updated' by purchasing them from somewhere outside the home.

But what happens to the gateway function of the set top box – its ability to stand guard over programme content and to get viewers to pay for it? This was the primary reason for which it was invented, after all.

The answer is that content ownership will get smarter. Audio and video material will come marked with proof of ownership embedded in digital code within the material. This code is rather like a series of digital watermarks. The home hub will work out from the digital watermark how much, if anything, is owed for viewing something and you will pay the provider – probably using some form of Internet-transmitted electronic money.

Already one large content owner, Viacom, is gearing up for providing a brave new world of home entertainment hubs. Viacom has signed a deal with IBM for the IT colossus to provide it with a system which holds content and then 're-purposes' it for many different types of media. Viacom's unified IT platform could support conception, creation, distribution and management of content by the end of seven years of development. The cost will be more than $500 million. It was announced on 7 May 2002.

The problem for Viacom is how to second-guess where the helter-skelter ride with media – produced by serving up advanced digital transmission to a generation which wants to experiment – will take the digital television industry. Will they simply want to plug in a personal receiving device, download clips of their favourite comic and take it off with them down the pub to show their mates? Whatever they want to do, Viacom has to try to be ready for it.

For example, a clip might come into Viacom which is shot in analogue: this must be converted to a digital file for editing, converted and compressed for digital transmission, and then converted separately for all possible screen resolutions for use on the Internet[41] (your computer currently has eight). Viacom has to think of a content factory if it is to keep pace with the relentless demands posed by how the young might use its MTV brand. What, then, will the MTV brand have at its core? A multimedia content factory, trying to reach its audiences on any device which technicians throw up and which the young will buy.

Old and deadly adversaries Microsoft and Apple are manoeuvring for position ahead of the anticipated digital hub war. Sony's Xbox game machine is designed to talk to a digital hub which can download new games over broadband connections into the Internet. The new Windows XP operating system is designed to distribute content, of whatever type, to devices and smart monitors around the home through a wireless connection.[42] The age of the hub in the house, distributing content to many different devices, is creeping nearer. Apple's iMac computer is similarly designed as a digital hub for the home that connects video and stills cameras, and also CD and DVD players.

This is one technological development which is likely to happen, as all the pressures from the groups who now use and watch television are towards:

- Getting exactly what they want when they want it (mainly driven by the lifestyles of the affluent)
- Linking similar content across as many media as possible (mainly driven by the young).

Dr Graham Wallace, Network Development Director of cutting-edge television company Kingston Communications plc, is enthusiastic about the potential for home hubs:

> My belief is that home hubs will take off. But I don't think we're going to get there for a few years. I doodle around doing little diagrams of what might be in the home and what might be connected to what, and it becomes a morass of wires and bits

and pieces very rapidly. If you look at it and if you've got an interactive connection through cable or DSL, you'll have a load of storage, you'll want to connect to your hi-fi, you'll want to take audio files off the Internet, you'll want to play DVDs . . . and play games. You rapidly end up with a home server which is basically only a PC sitting under the stairs and some sort of local network in the house. That's where I think people will end up. But I think it will take a while for a significant percentage of the population to get there.

The creation of hubs means an end to a distinct device in the corner around which the family sit watching channels. That was a version of family behaviour that died with analogue transmission, and with the unreasonable demands of the affluent and the young on entertainment technology.

The simple diagram in Figure 3 shows how the home of the future will be fed by the large content creation and re-purposing systems which Viacom has started to build with IBM. This will mark the end of the set top box, as in such a system with a very intelligent hub you will no longer have a single cheap device attached to the television enabling it to receive digital.

More importantly, it will stimulate further changes in the way in which households are entertained and receive information. It will

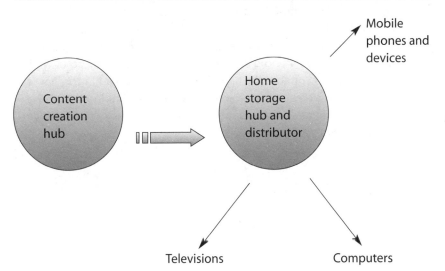

Figure 4.3. The end of the set top box and the end of the family around the television

encourage people to behave more as single individuals, with distinct tastes and viewing personalities. It will mean the end of family viewing – and pose broadcasters major problems in identifying and satisfying the audiences of the future.

Jas Saini on home hubs

Jas Saini is Vice President of Consumer Appliances at the world's leading supplier of software for set top boxes, NDS. He believes in the vision that digital hubs will dominate the home – but also cautions that the idea has been around a long time:

Fifteen years ago we were looking at home devices: home networks based on a central hub. But in those days we had one massive problem – television. If you wanted to pipe television around the house you couldn't do it because we didn't have compression technology. Now we've got the ability to compress the data we can do it many ways – through a wireless network, or even through the telephone lines – so it is going to happen. I don't think it's going to happen this year, or even next year. I think it's going to take about three or four years.

In three or four years, people will have Personal Video Recorder type boxes (see Chapter 9). Now that lends itself very well to be the central hub. So it could come in through a back door through a product like that. You start with one of our 'XTV' boxes and you extend it.

NDS has been looking at that because the problem with all of these devices around the house is you're going to have to encrypt the signal – scramble it – because it's no different to sending it along any other wire. A pirate could de-scramble the signal and steal it. So within the home you're going to have to encrypt it somehow. This is technology which we have been looking at. We have done a lot of work already on this. We've shown some things at shows.

Making Production Pay

THREE-WAY IMPACT

Digital television has greatly increased the ability of broadcasters to deliver many channels, and even the exact programme the viewer desires, directly into the home. This has dealt programme makers a blow from which many of them are still recovering. The effects of digital – and particularly its economics – seem to them strange and arbitrary. In fact, they are inescapable. The main effects of digital technology on programme makers have been:

- To force down the price which ordinary programme makers are paid for their product
- To make the pursuit of the 'hit' series an absolute priority, pursued by the big studios and the main channels
- To make commissioners think about programmes and channels as scientific *types* with specific values and characteristics.

The first effect, forcing down the price of television programming, seems counter-intuitive to many programme makers. If there are more channels, and more programmes required to fill them, surely the amount of money spent on programming will go up? However, most independent production companies know the truth. In the digital era their profitability has fallen drastically – often to a level where a 2 per cent margin is a good return. There are three reasons for this:

1. The growth of digital channels has severely damaged the monopolies of the old terrestrial networks. They have less money to spend as their revenues have been challenged. This leads inexorably to the second and third reasons . . .
2. More producers are now working as small independents, and not as employees of the old monopolies. This happened as broadcasters shed costs and became commissioning organisations.

The people they shed were the programme makers who, outside of the protection of a large organisation, were dictated to by the commissioning broadcasters on pricing. No independent is likely to say – 'that's too low a price – I just can't make it for that'. They will strive to make it for a low price and sacrifice their profit margin, simply in order to pay themselves a wage and stay in the business. Many independents in the digital age make a loss and depend on deep-pocketed backers who are waiting for them to come up with a hit series.

3. The increased competition between the multiplicity of channels means that the average cost of 80 per cent of programming will fall as new channels, unlike the old monopolies, will fill their schedules using the 'eighty/twenty rule'. This dictates that eighty per cent of programming is there simply to supply the 'feel' and brief of the channel when hardly anyone is watching: twenty per cent is there in order to deliver large audiences, and is where the majority of broadcasters' budgets are spent. The times at which large audiences are available varies with the brief of the channel. With children's channels it is weekends and early evening; with news channels it is early morning.

'Hit' programme scheduling is not new – but what is new is the rigorous enforcement of its economic logic. Instead of giving a large group of programme makers a decent living, independent of whether their programmes were hits or not, the digital television universe will do anything to produce and grab rights for 'hits', while they will pay as near as next to nothing as they can for the production of the rest of the schedule.

This makes being an independent producer an uncomfortable experience – unless you can produce a hit.

However, it is possible to be a rich independent producer in the world of digital television. This can happen in one of two ways, if independents:

■   Hold important rights, either to talent or programme formats which broadcasters can't obtain anywhere else.
■   Deliver a hit series. When it becomes a hit they may not hold the rights initially, but if they are shrewd the rights and the talent involved will gradually leach away over time to the independent producer.

Holding onto rights is easier said than done. Broadcasters will do almost anything to keep important rights to transmission in their own hands. So, for example, if a network commissions a documentary series it will oblige the producer to give it domestic transmission rights in perpetuity. Networks often concede the overseas rights in factual series to producers, as the costs of exploiting them are so high as to make their sale uneconomic. But if a series, particularly a game show format, suddenly becomes unexpectedly successful then overseas rights can become very valuable.

The sure-fire way to hold broadcasters to ransom on rights is to own human 'talent'. Typically this is in the form of someone who has already become famous through television – like Oprah Winfrey or Rowan Atkinson. Atkinson set up *Tiger Aspect Productions* quite early in his career. It has now expanded beyond comedies featuring him to drama featuring other people. There is now a very fine dividing line between running a talent agency and independent production. If you own the talent why not package it into a show, so that the broadcaster only has to sign a programme commission to get it on screen?

HITS

One of the most fascinating of all entertainment product phenomena is the 'hit'. Hits are programmes – normally series – which achieve a mass following, and also that elusive and valuable thing: a brand.

Hits are very important as they provide people with a strong reason to tune to a particular channel or to pay to watch a programme. In kicking off its new digital channel, E4, the UK's Channel 4 showed the latest episodes of *Ally McBeal* and *ER*. This had the effect of at least getting people to sample that channel.

Some channels are little more than delivery conduits for two or three hit shows. Nickelodeon is so dependent on *Keenan and Kel* and *Sabrina the Teenage Witch* that often all it does is play these shows back to back. However, Nickelodeon would argue that these shows fit perfectly with the channel's remit at the time of writing, and when they become unpopular or irrelevant to it they will air other shows.

Hits are therefore incredibly valuable. Anything that starts as a humble series and then migrates to hit status tends to pull profit towards itself, and out of whatever part of the television supply chain in which it previously resided. In recent history this has happened with the casts of both *Friends* and *Frasier* – in each case the network has needed the series to keep its audience, but the actual talent perform very tough negotiations as the price of making yet another series. Ultimately this has the effect that the networks make little or no profit out of the series. It all goes in costs – and notably in the stars' salaries.

Hits are such an important component of digital television broadcasting that the skill involved in creating them is gradually assuming the status of a science. Peter Martin,[43] in a ground-breaking piece of work, has worked out what it takes to be successful in the hits business:

- *Feeding the machine.* It is important to have a talent acquisition machine that gets a reasonable share of new talent at an acceptable cost. One of the weaknesses of the new digital broadcasters is that they are over-reliant on independent producers and traditional broadcasters for new talent.
- *Managing the hype.* Knowing how and when to push artists who display signs of turning into real stars. This also goes for shows and series, which often do not perform well on a first run. Powerful networks are good at cross-promoting new shows and talent – but if the audience has no appetite for them then the effort and resource will be wasted. So quick decisions about who and what to promote are essential.
- *Killing off the losers.* The converse to hype is knowing when to drop a series, or a performer who isn't going to be a star.
- *Holding onto the winners.* The challenge here is that most shows which become hits are contracted on terms which are at first very advantageous to the broadcaster. Eventually, as the hit takes off, the stars will renegotiate their contracts. But the longer the period of the initial contract can be extended the more profitable will be the relationship for the broadcaster. This involves charm, guile and flattery.

If all this sounds vaguely amoral, it indicates the way in which digital technology is driving broadcasting executives to behave. What is required for success is a mixture of personal charisma and complete emotional ruthlessness.

Walt Disney wrestles with hit-production day to day. It is the nature of its business. Recently the business has been demonstrating why you can never stand still when developing hits. *Who Wants To Be A Millionaire* (a format bought from Celador of the UK) was the mainstay of Disney's ABC network, but is now declining in popularity. It needs to be replaced. But on Disney's movie side they have managed to innovate and produce *Monsters Inc*, the smash hit of 2002, in partnership with computer animators Pixar.

Hits and declining shows are impossible to predict: hence the expression that in the ultimate hit factory, Hollywood, 'no one knows anything'. But because of the importance of hits to its business – and notably to its spreading portfolio of digital television channels – Disney treats the creation of hits very scientifically. Paul Robinson is Vice President in charge of programme content worldwide for Disney's television channels. He says:

> There is a bit of a roll of the dice in creating content. You don't get a six every time. So you have to invest, and to accept that some things won't work. We do that every year – we commission a number of series and some things are cancelled. We've just cancelled a series called *Bob Patterson* with ABC in the States, which was one of the new fall series which didn't work out. The trick is knowing when to get off.
>
> It is completely about risk management – if you win, you win big, and you earn many times over your investment. But you're hedging the whole way. First of all you get an idea, then you get a 'bible' (a book which describes the concept). Then you get a script. Then you do a short five-minute animation. You then research that, discuss it and get feedback widely. You then might go to a pilot or a short run. But you wouldn't then renew the first run until you had gone through the whole process again with audience research.

Hits are essential to get people to watch a channel. Even in the early days of digital no one has seriously tried to overthrow the primacy of the channel as the means of delivering television content to an audience. Technology is offering several alternatives, which are dealt with later in this book.

But there are many more channels than there used to be, simply because digital transmission allows it. This has made it important that channels have distinct identities that stick out in the minds of potential audiences. Giving a product, like a channel, an identity has led to serious thinking about channels as brands. It has also necessitated trying to work out what kinds of programmes are needed to give a channel a different look and feel from another channel. This has led to the philosophy of television programme 'genres' or types. To keep up with the present generation of television executives a firm grasp of the idea of 'genres' is obligatory.

Being successful in a genre

There are downsides to being too successful as an independent producer. Celador, the production company which makes *Who Wants To Be A Millionaire*, has discovered several of them. The first is that inventing the greatest mass-audience show of recent memory created an enormous burden to come up with the next one. Paul Smith, the founder of Celador, is investing £2 million a year in coming up with new entertainment ideas. He admits that the chances of creating another *Millionaire* are small.

The second problem is that most of the mass ratings channels' situations are now so dire that, if they are gifted with a hit, they will over-expose it. ABC in the States became highly dependent on the show but, as Smith says, 'scheduled *Millionaire* into the ground, completely ruthlessly. It was on air virtually continuously for two years, four or five days a week. What other show would survive that kind of exposure?'

But *Millionaire* has made Smith enough to retire on. It is licensed in more than 60 countries.[44]

GENRES AND BRANDS

The development of programme genres came with the decline of the old network monopolies. Channel owners needed a tool which allowed them to build a channel schedule and calculate quickly if they were getting value for money. As many of the new digital channels would be run on a shoestring it was important for them to get appropriate material quickly to give a channel a distinct identity at an appropriate price.

This led to programmes being divided up into genres. So, for example, there are about three genres of drama: feature length drama, drama series and soap operas. Feature length drama is going to be more expensive per hour than soap opera because soaps occupy a great deal of time, and so the cost per episode is lower than that for one-offs.

Genres are useful. Clearly a 'Lifestyle' channel (designed to appeal to women) will only contain certain genres of programming, such as made for TV movies, sofa based chat and factual programming about health. Once a programme controller has defined the precise mix of these shows that they want, it is easy for the accountants to work out how much it should all cost to make. The programme controller will then attempt to commission the best and most original programmes in the genres. Typically there will not be enough programmes to give the channel controller an overwhelming advantage over other channels, as they will not be able to afford to commission new original material which is aimed at the target audience. Furthermore, even if they can do this they will not have the budgets to afford to get the original material right first time. This gives programme-commissioning machines like Disney's an overwhelming advantage, as they can afford to spread the costs of original commissioning over many channels worldwide.

The relationship between commissioning, creativity and the benchmarking of genres emerges in the way in which Paul Robinson talks about the risks inherent in commissioning programming:

> You start with the idea, but then there are a number of filters. One would be audience. Another would be genre. Do we want live action? Do we want drama? Do we want animation? Another would be cost. There are benchmarks for every genre. Another would be deciding who is going to make these films. It's an interesting mix of analysis and creativity. At the end of the day you can do the research and the analysis but you've got to make a call. And that's where the risk comes in. Because you could make a call which didn't happen to fit the mood of the public at that time. Look at September 11. A number of movies that were good calls pre-September 11 are now bad calls. We had one live action movie with a scene in New York which has been delayed rather than pulled.

WHY BOTHER WITH CHANNELS?

Digital has changed the way in which channels are constructed and the way they look and feel. The economics of the new technology has forced these changes. The practical effect of commissioning programmes so that 80 per cent of the budget is spent on a few hit shows is that:

- Digital channels have a very closely defined programming mix
- They are very reliant on a few hit shows.

This shows up starkly if the top ten shows for the average digital channel are compared by audience size.

Top programmes on 'Living', week ending 19 August 2001	Size of audience
Jerry Springer compilation	180,000
Charmed	170,000
Jerry Springer	170,000
Ricki Lake	160,000
Jerry Springer	150,000
Jerry Springer	150,000
Jerry Springer compilation	140,000
Passion Cove	130,000
Maury Povich	120,000
Girlfriends	120,000

Table 5.1. The top ten shows on 'Living' during one week in August 2001

The plain fact is that 'Living' would be sunk without the *Jerry Springer Show*, which is contributing most of its audience peaks.

Digital technology has capabilities and potential which were not present in the old analogue form of broadcasting. As discussed in Chapter 1, with a certain amount of adaptation it can deliver 'programmes on demand' – as and when the viewer wants to see them. So why – when a channel is serving an audience which essentially is obsessed with *Jerry Springer* – bother to deliver a channel at all? Why not simply deliver *Jerry Springer* on demand and abandon the notion of a channel?

Broadcasters are very resistant to this notion. It is very easy to view this as broadcasters staying within the traditional comfort zone of their upbringing. But most of them advance some compelling arguments for still using channels, even to deliver what on most digital channels is a very narrow range of programming. Paul Robinson argues it this way:

> While I would agree that, going forward, people are going to be drawn to compelling content, they still want to have someone help

them to make a decision. The problem with having all the content available is that it is like having a menu in a restaurant with 500 main courses. The fact that they exist is not very useful to you. What you actually want is for them to give you a selection of ten courses from which you choose. I think TV's not dissimilar. I believe that people in ten or twenty years' time will still use TV principally as a medium for entertainment, a sit-back medium, so that's about making it easy. I think the challenge is about letting people sit back and say to the television, 'entertain me'. If every decision has to be complicated and measured, I think that makes it hard for people to consume. I think the net result of that would be that consumption would actually drop.

If you look at the increased supply of channels in multi-channel households, this has now increased with 60 channels more than viewers used to have with analogue. The number of channels which people actually watch has not grown with increased supply. They still have a repertoire of ten or twelve channels. What additional channels do is give you increased tailoring and increased choice. There's more likely to be a channel for you.

For all those reasons I think that people will continue to use channels, as people then can still consume TV in an easy, linear, passive way.

Paul's point is that channels have an identity of their own which is separate from the programming they carry – if people switch to them hoping to be entertained, they will be entertained in a way in which they expect. This is because entertainment is a very subjective experience, and is to do with 'feel'. What audiences find relaxing and diverting is likely to differ greatly across different demographics. As such, the type of entertainment a person desires can be defined by the 'feel' of a brand – in this case 'Lifestyle'. This is embodied in the channel: in its identity, its promotions, its presentation and all the cheap programming which it carries when the peak shows aren't running. You don't know if you will get *Jerry Springer* in 2001, but you know you will probably get something like it – 'home based' issues done in a way in which you can't miss them.

However with the advance of technologies such as broadband it becomes easier simply to give people exactly the shows they want – and over the Internet. Isn't it better for the makers of *Jerry Springer* that they deliver their programmes straight into the home via broadband and don't have channel controllers taking their cut of the subscriptions that the shows are generating?

Disney believe that this argument falls down if the featured programme genres are essentially entertainment – as people watch entertainment in a different frame of mind from information programmes.

> I believe that people who have broadband Internet will use it. It is like a tap – you can turn it on and find out about shopping, sport or whatever. I would distinguish the TV from the PC in terms of usage – I think the PC is principally going to be about information, while the TV is principally going to be about entertainment. Broadband will have a fundamental impact upon the Internet. As far as TV is concerned, it will allow all kinds of content pushes and pulls from consumers. I think there will be all kinds of opportunities to do creative things with television by virtue of these wide 'pipes', but I don't think that will substitute completely for conventional, laid-back, passive TV. I think it will be an add-on which will be a function of genre – so news and sport will be the obvious ones, as well as financial news and travel news. You can already get movies on demand through digital TV. The thing about broadband is the return path – and there will be occasions when people want to engage. But that's more about their mood, about how they feel. If you are tired, you simply want to be entertained.
>
> (Paul Robinson)

There are, however, weaknesses in the notion of the 'entertainment' channel. An obvious one is that programme controllers distrust the idea that not everyone has identical tastes in entertainment. Although it is a simple rule of marketing that not everyone likes the same thing, this has always seemed to be a brave notion in television. A few years ago 'reality TV' ('filming ordinary people under stress' is a good catch-all definition) didn't exist. But when entertainment networks (like ABC or ITV) found that it seemed to catch a nerve with the audiences of the late nineties, suddenly it was everywhere.

There is a compelling reason why this happens – often controllers, even with a budget to commission original programming, do not have a budget to cover risk and innovation. This leads to similarities between programmes which are trying to entertain – it is safer to tell your shareholders that you are producing types of programming which work for other channels than to report that you have identified a niche audience who you *think* want to be entertained but who no-one is serving.

This scarcity of money to spend on programming leads to a natural constraint in the growth of digital channels. As there is only a finite audience for television, the only thing which determines whether or not your channel will get a higher audience than anyone else's is the amount of risk you can take on developing programming which is outstandingly good. Disney has a vast programme-making machine. They have defined themselves as a company which does this: programme making, not distribution, is their core activity.

They have done this partly because they believe that creating more channels *ad infinitum* leads to an impossible universe. It is simply not possible to keep adding channels so that people will splinter into smaller and smaller groups until everyone gets programmes made for them as individuals. The economics of programme production does not allow it.

> There's no significant reduction in the amount of time people spend watching television. It's still about 24–26 hours a week – one day a week. The cake has grown very slightly – but the game for digital channel operators is essentially about taking share from terrestrial broadcasters. The question is 'what is the endgame there?' Because there comes a point where you over-supply the market and end up with a number of channels which are rather thin in content, because the economics of the business don't support rich content, and therefore you don't get a good audience. I think there is an argument that there is a point at which the number of channels reaches a limit.

This theory suggests that eventually, in the digital age, television will be supplied by a finite number of reasonably well-funded channels.

But neither the technologists nor the marketeers believe this. Their disagreement with the likes of Disney means that investment in new forms of digital continues, and the uncertainty engendered by television's digital revolution gets worse.

CHAPTER 6

Watch Out America: You're Next!

NEW PROGRAMMES FOR NEW AUDIENCES

Chapter 2 portrayed the habits of the new audience as a challenge to platform owners – as their technology struggled to keep pace with the increasing and unreasonable demands of their viewers. However there is another series of problems just as big for content makers. They have to find answers to the following questions:

- Is there any kind of mass audience channel (or programme) which this audience will watch?
- What will be the big hit shows of the future?
- In what form should their content be transmitted? Is it possible to have a 'show' whose primary content is not a television programme at all, but in fact is other forms of electronic content distributed over digital television?

The problem is becoming more acute in the USA with the spread of digital television: 16.7 million out of 105.5 million US homes get digital cable television. It was zero in 1997. Another 17.6 million homes get digital TV through satellite broadcasters.[45] That's 32 per cent of US homes and climbing. America's still behind the UK and France (at 39 per cent). However, the European experience shows that the US market will rapidly come under pressure from the challenges and threats which digital transmission engenders.

Some examples of those pressures that are now hitting the US are as follows:

- The mass channels are haemorrhaging audience share
- Some of the biggest hits are advertised by word of mouth through digital devices, and have television audiences which are minute compared with their social impact

- Young, cheeky entrepreneurs are using new technology to undercut digital cable prices.

The last point is the most disconcerting – particularly as cable networks in the US are charging between $70 and $90 a month for digital services (compared with average packages of $45 in the UK). So entrepreneurs are finding ways to use the technology against the big providers. Phil Goldman, who co-founded WebTV Networks, has created Total TV. It uses a cheap set top box and transmits digital signals to the ordinary aerial on the rooftop. If this sounds like digital terrestrial television which, state owned and awarded, had such a disastrous ride in Europe, that's exactly what it is. But in America the market finds a use for technology – and with cable networks overcharging, the market is creating an opportunity for terrestrial broadcasters. All Mr Goldman has to do is to get the necessary licences off the Federal Communications Commission. Phil Goldman says that 'if Total TV can win these auctions, it has everything it needs to start broadcasting nationwide'.[46]

The most pressing problem the US networks face is that their audience is voting with its selector switches. ABC's prime time network audience fell by 23 per cent overall to just 9.7 million viewers in 2002, and the decline in the essential 18–49 year old audience was an equally catastrophic 18 per cent. To stem the flow ABC has pressed the panic button, and ordered an extraordinary 29 new comedy and drama pilots. Their analysis of the problem has concluded that they have no new hot shows. But this analysis is simplistic.

Fox's ratings also dropped 11 per cent among the 18–49 year old audience this season.[47] Fox's remedy has been to commission new shows and to install many of them at 8 in the evening. Again, this is classic traditional network thinking. It will get them nowhere.

But within the US television market there are glimmers that some operators now understand that audiences are demanding channels which seem to be tailor-made for them. For example, recent new channels and channel concepts to emerge include the following:

- Discovery Wings (for aviation enthusiasts).
- Viacom is studying plans for a gay TV channel; in fact there is one already, from a Canadian company called Pridevision.
- EW Scripps has launched the DIY Channel and Fine Living networks.

This shows awareness that new audiences want something which appears to be personally made for them. The most interesting phenomenon of the new US television season is the success of the show which adorns every US magazine cover but was watched by one of the lowest television audiences ever recorded: the documentary by MTV about Ozzy Osbourne and his wacky family.

HOW TO GET NEW AUDIENCES

What lessons can worried US broadcasting executives draw from this? The clues to what works and why are already being road-tested in the European digital television market. The big lesson is in the behaviour of the young, who have adopted the attitude of the affluent early adopters of digital television and have taken their logic to new extremes. The most important feature in the young's use of digital television is that they are prepared to consume television technology in ways that were never intended. This is a common but often-forgotten characteristic of new technology: it is rarely used as it was intended, and the group most prepared to experiment will push it to its extremes. A simple example is the separate 'interactive' area on digital television. It was envisaged this would be accessed through its own gateway, and used as a service which often had little relationship with the main television channels. This model fell apart when young users rapidly took to making links between a television programme and the interactive area of the set top box. So much so that most users now access interactivity via a television channel, and not through the 'official' interactive gateway. This is entirely logical: why would an audience which wants 'exactly what it wants when it wants it' bother to go looking for it? But suggest that the best moments from the game you are watching can be seen by pressing a red button now and people will migrate, for a few minutes, to an interactive area.

This chapter gives the basic rules which will be followed by the victors in the digital television battle – and supports this with an analysis of the way in which the new viewers use digital television for their benefit.

The basic rules for success for grabbing digital television audience are straightforward:

- Make content which is personal (or seems to be personal) to your audience.

- Appear to give them exactly what they want, when they want it.

- Don't try to create hit shows: only do shows which start as cults in certain communities. The instant hit will become increasingly unattainable.

- Stop trying to appeal to a mass audience: it will become almost impossible to plan new channels or new shows in this way.

- Try to involve the audience emotionally in the shows, using aspects of the new technology.

- Be mindful that there is money to be made from editioning and archiving, and also from other forms of content.

- Remember that you are creating an electronic brand – not a television programme.

These rules are the core of this book. The rest of the book explores how they are being followed by successful operators, or ignored by the failing ones. Taking each rule in turn . . .

Make content which is personal to your audience

Successful platform operators strive to do this as they know this gives them the ability to meet the demands of the new 'unreasonable' audience. However, much digital television personalisation is an illusion – the economics of platforms mean that it is prohibitively expensive to allow a viewer to draw down a film off a distant play out centre exactly when they want it. No platform operator who is allowing viewers to draw down content on demand from a play out centre is currently making money out of this.

Satellite television has solved this problem with 'Near Video on Demand' – films starting at half-hour intervals to allow viewers to access them at a time of their choosing. On BSkyB in the UK, and DirecTV in the US, the most popular film of the day occupies eight channels and starts at quarter-hour intervals.

New boxes incorporate a hard disc which allows the box to record programmes, and then waits for the viewer to be able to watch them. With clever software, this allows the viewer to assert their other great demand: having what they want.

Give them exactly what they want, when they want it

Successful operators are developing set top box technology that monitors an individual's viewing habits, and then stores and hides content so that it appears to be there exactly when they want it. This is what the TiVo box does, using a personal rating system. The TiVo box knows what kind of programmes you prefer; it then goes ahead and records programmes which it decides are likely to appeal to you. This makes huge demands on the TiVo operation: all programmes have to labelled and categorised so that the TiVo box knows enough about the programmes to act as an automatic (and highly personalised) 'digital television shopping assistant'. However, the economics are radically cheaper from those of true 'on-demand' television, where the viewer calls down content from a distant play out centre.

There are other ways of making the digital television experience appear entirely personal: for example, by ensuring that the national channel you are watching is a variation for your particular region, subtly mixing regional and national content without the viewer being aware of the geographical tailoring involved. All the methods used by successful operators for content personalisation are dealt with in Chapter 9.

Don't try to create hit shows

This is going to be an extremely hard lesson for broadcasters to learn. It is almost counter-intuitive to a broadcaster not to try to design a hit from stage one – everyone watches hits, don't they? In the world of digital television, viewers (and particularly young viewers) watch something which is about them or their community. This means that the way to get to a hit is to start with a cult. Cults are cheap to make and can easily be tested out using other electronic media.

The problem with the hit format was that it was always something of an illusion. A show which everyone watched relied on a serendipitous combination of a broad appeal to a mass audience and being on the right channel at the right time. Peter Bazalgette, one of the most successful producers of hit factual programmes in Europe, makes clear how random the process of hit creation really is:

Everytime we start a new idea that we hope will amuse people, we make a pilot. It's like having a nervous breakdown, basically – like looking down into a very deep abyss, questioning everything you know and asking 'do I know anything at all about what people want?' You never know if it's going to work or not. All you can do is use your collective knowledge – and you have as many failures as you have successes. I wouldn't like to tell you about one or two of the pilots I've made this year which have been complete disasters. I think we have learnt new tricks. We've learnt to format programmes more – and we've learnt to make them interactive. You can do what Michael Jackson[48] was good at, which is to put his nose to the wind. When he asked me to invent *Changing Rooms* he said 'Can you do me a DIY show for the evenings, like *Ready Steady Cook* combined with *Home Front* (which is a magazine show)?' so I invented *Changing Rooms* on that basis. He had somehow divined that there was this interest in spending money on the home. It goes quite deep, this emotion about home and what the home represents. It was an instinct and it proved right. And other instincts of his proved wrong. So having people who have good instincts around is important. I don't think I've got them, actually, as I don't read magazines and I never read a tabloid newspaper. My inspiration is based on a stimulus – but someone has to give that to me.

The fact of the matter is that there is a much quicker and cheaper way to build hit programmes in the world of digital television – this is to create viral cults.

The viral cult owes something both to the young and to the way in which they use the new technology. It is in essence a programme, game or piece of software whose fame is spread by electronic world of mouth. The electronic games industry is the most virulent example of this phenomenon, with e-mails, newsgroups and web sites which tell players about the latest releases – and even how to cheat at them.

Now that television has become just another extension of the world of digital content, it has become susceptible to this approach. For example, there are now newsgroups available on the Internet discussing cult shows. A newsgroup is a collection of e-mails from people who have a topic or interest in common.

They can be very useful (for example, sharing ways in which to fix problems with Windows 98) and are a long-established part of Internet culture. Applied to digital television, their effect is devastating.

Here is one message from the States to a newsgroup devoted to the subject of the Dutch-owned show *Big Brother*:

> When will *BB3* start in the US?
> > I keep watching out for advertisements and I've saw a few that just say
> > *BB3* Comming Soon, But I wanna know when. I have yet to miss an episode
> > of any *BB* shows. Im getting so excited about it Dose anyone know
> > when????

They got the answer 'May 5' from someone in Europe.

In other words, followers of the show are not reliant on published schedules or the television for information: they get it from people in other countries whom they meet on the Internet.

Equally, it is possible to get a new show talked about on television Internet sites – or sites devoted to programmes that attract people who are likely to watch a new show. This is very close to what advertisers have identified as the most powerful advertising medium in the world: 'word of mouth'. If your mates recommend it, it is sure to be good. This reflects a curious illusion embodied in the newsgroup – people appear to be your mates, part of your community, but in reality you hardly know anything about them. However, because of the feeling that they are 'people like you' you trust them.

This is how shows like the documentary about Ozzy Osbourne, the dysfunctional pop star, are becoming famous even though the initial television ratings are very low. It is much cheaper to make a show, or even a pilot series, which gets talked about on other electronic chat media and then invest a lot of money in a follow-up, than in gearing up for the production of piloting 'hits'. If it does well as a viral cult, it is worth pursuing. Just watch, on other media, what the audience makes of it. The newsgroups certainly told MTV that they had a hit series which they could sell to the main networks. Here is a typical e-mail from *The Osbournes'* newsgroup:

ok, sounds corny, but....I am going thru osbournes with-
drawals!!
LOL

They tapes 13 episodes, 10 get played, 3 are still out there,
and they say they are putting together 1 more for a total
of 4 that we havn't seen yet.

I still have to wait 3 more months before I get to see him
in concert live in the center front row! :o)

Damn, its going to be a Looooooong wait.

–

BuZZard

It is both expensive and difficult to pursue hits. It may be better
to build them from cults. The technology allows broadcasters
to do this (and to monitor the process). It has to be more effective and cheaper than the agonising and random process that
Peter Bazalgette describes. But broadcasters trust their
instincts – and so the wasteful habit will take a long time to
kick.

Stop trying to appeal to a mass audience

The figures which illustrate the decline of mass audience channels
are given at the beginning of this Chapter and in Chapter 7 (which
examines the impact on advertising). Broadcasters, however, often
mistakenly see increased competition as the main cause of this,
and not the fact that it is now remarkably difficult to get a very
large group of people to act and react in a similar manner to
anything. This is because we are too time-pressured and too
tightly scheduled, and are bringing up a generation which has
adopted these values as a form of apolitical ideology (as is
explained later in the chapter).

The simple fact of the matter is that shows designed to appeal
to huge audiences will become increasingly ineffective because
people no longer want the same things – in fact, they define
themselves as *not* wanting what the person next door wants.
What will be feasible in the future will be to take a common piece

of electronic content (or branding) and re-version it in many different ways, so that it appeals to many audiences. But to have one huge audience watching one single piece of media is an increasingly unattainable goal. It is a waste of money and resources to attempt it.

Try to involve the audience emotionally

Peter Bazalgette has already talked about the need to engage the new, promiscuous, channel-hopping audiences with emotional 'hooks'. The new technology allows viewers to feel that they are involved in a show, and can in some small way determine either its output or the way it is directed, by allowing the audience to select cameras and shots.

Using technology to encourage you to interact with a show (and to talk about it on the web) is being pioneered by channel owners who have to appeal to a young audience. Experimenting with early set top boxes taught MTV that it was possible to make their hit interactive show *Video Clash*. Simon Guild of MTV Networks Europe explains how it works:

> We screened a show in the UK last year called *Video Clash*. The principle of the show is that you have two videos on the screen. One video was playing: there are two heads, one on either side of the screen with a name underneath each, and you vote for one or the other. And it interacts directly with the technology. So the percentages update dynamically and you vote with SMS. You vote and send a message, and we'll play a selection of messages. At the end of the show, at the end of the previous video the winner out of the two – the one with the biggest percentage – is then chosen and the programme cuts to that video. This is technically quite complicated to arrange, as you can probably imagine. But we pulled it off, and we're now doing it in most countries in Europe.

This kind of 'emotional technology strategy' is far more effective with the young than even with the affluent (who simply demand that the technology saves them time and gives them what they want). But the young have no pre-conceptions about how television should work, and are prepared to watch shows where outcomes can be determined by the viewer.

The peculiar appeal of digital television technology to the young is analysed later in this chapter.

There is money to be made from editioning and archiving

If mass audiences cannot be reached through one medium, it follows that there will be money to made from programme brands which can be re-editioned and archived. A good example of this is news, where news operations like *The Wall Street Journal*, *The Financial Times* and the BBC have all created online modes of distribution (in addition to their primary means of news provision): all of those have an archive as a major feature. In fact, online archived material is so valuable that it is almost a medium in its own right. Both *The Financial Times* and *The Wall Street Journal* have started charging for access to their online archives.

Furthermore, all future developments in set top box architecture point to more use of personal archives and choice. It is pointless set top boxes asking you about personal favourites if they cannot meet your needs from a vast programme archive. The debate now is how programmes could, and should, be categorised to meet this call for archived material – which the technology is encouraging and the audience is demanding.

In the future no-one is going to get poor by owning the rights to complete series of old hit shows – particularly US ones. In addition, more and more production companies will install expensive systems that re-purpose television material over several media, like the system Viacom has just commissioned from IBM.

Remember you are creating an electronic brand

Television, as a powerful medium, is still good at giving impetus to an idea. However, it is getting worse at coming up with an initial idea which a lot of people will watch. That is why this book argues that the best way to fine-tune an idea is to see if it takes off in a particular community. Yet television will still be an essential ingredient in boosting the new idea's profile and values once it has taken off: in other words, establishing its brand.

Nevertheless, once an electronic brand is established it can, and will, spread to many media. Even television 'conservatives' like Jim Hytner see this in their vision of the digital future, which has old television channels as the core medium in a universe of proliferating media:

> My view, slightly controversially, is that everything will still start with television. SMS texting is popular because of the shows the young watch. Because there is something they want to vote for from a television. You go on the Internet to get the newspapers; then they are going to be reading the front pages about, for example, our show *Pop Idol*. And *Pop Idol* is a television show. I still think that television shows feed the chat, and from that comes other media that the young consume. I still believe that last Wednesday we attracted 15 per cent of all 16–24s in the country with the Brit Awards.
>
> Now this is in the new era. This is in the new world. This is in the world of Internet and of SMS texting. The world of digital media. It's in the world of 16–24s being as promiscuous as ever and yet one programme – and the media associated with it – is still attracting half the population of 16–24 year olds.

However, Jim Hytner is describing a mass audience phenomenon which is based on a 16–24 cult – and owes a lot of its audience reach to being available on many different media simultaneously. The world of hit shows and peak viewing has truly changed.

THE NEW AUDIENCE: STRONG OPINIONS, LIGHTLY HELD

The audiences of the future pose a profound problem to digital broadcasters. How do you plan programmes, services, or even new media if the generation adopting them shows no tendency to watch television as its parents did? Worse, give them a new technology and they immediately come up with new ways of using it. They are:

- *Promiscuous:* they range and sample across all media with confidence, even those with which they are unfamiliar.
- *Headliners:* they will absorb headline messages and very quickly move on. They won't stay to concentrate unless they find the content utterly compelling.
- *They want exactly what they want, when they want it:* they

behave as if they are subject to the same time pressures as the affluent.

This last characteristic is the strangest. Why would young viewers, who have leisure time, behave as if they don't? The answer to this involves the revelation that the young are driven by an image of themselves that already has them as time-pressured adults. However, the difference is that they are time-pressured, *technologically confident* adults. This means that they will try anything – any format, any combination of technology – in order to relieve their *imaginary time pressure*. The importance of this is that it makes it almost impossible to predict either what they will view or how they will view it.

Sid McGrath is paid to understand the young. As Planning Director of advertising agency HHCL, he has to try to tell clients how to get young consumers to accept new brands. But since this generation is setting the pace (and the style) of how the new communications technology is used, this is a severe challenge. How do you tell a generation what to watch when they are re-defining how 'watching' should be done?

> The new generation demands that the price of entry brings instantaneous content, without having to wait around for it. 'I want to watch it – I want to watch it now. I don't want to see the programme before. I want to see a specific programme now. I want it totally ordered around my life.' We've all read science fiction books where the world was tailored around our specific needs. I think there's a great insight there into a future where everything is ordered around your ego and your desires. I think that's what the young want to move towards; that's why digital TV will not only create content on demand but will also be forced to create content which is individualised to meet a person's specific needs.

This is tied up with the young deciding that they, like their parents, are time-pressured:

> Until broadband becomes the main method of communication download, people will remain tremendously frustrated with time. Time, it seems, is one of those things which people have decided they have less and less of – even the young. Our understanding

of the young is that they feel they have so many things they have to do that they don't have time. 'Give it to me now' – it's all about instant gratification. It's well exemplified by one of the brands we have here – Pot Noodle. A tasty food which is designed to fill your stomach quickly. Pot Noodle, like a lot of food brands now, say this is all about 'food on the go'. It's very popular with the young because they don't have time to sit around and wait for things to download. They want to seize the opportunity now, and probably then move quickly onto something else.

However, this new television generation doesn't want to view indis-
criminately, or watch content without substance – they want to use the electronic media as tools which they can use to fulfil ambitions:

Ten years ago everyone said the way to talk to the young is through MTV culture – that is, information overload. Your ads must have lots of fast cuts in them, because that's consistent with the way they view media messages because they watch MTV. What everyone forgot is that there had to be a core message, style had moved in over content. There was research in the States where in answer to the question 'Do you think you will fulfil your life's ambition?' one hundred per cent of people said 'Yes'. They have tremendous self-confidence. So a lot of this pressure comes from a notion that they have their ambition to fulfil and can't wait for a download, or whatever. They want it now, as they have to move on fast.

Nevertheless, this tremendous self-confidence comes with a strange deficit – the young have no strong or fixed opinions of their own. It has hard to say why this has happened. It could be the lack of real political controversy in the West since the collapse for communism. It could simply be because virulent consumer soci-
eties breed a lack of fixed beliefs – substituting a series of messages about brands. In fact the only fixed belief which some young opinion formers seem to have come up with in the last five years is that they don't like brands, although 'brands' are vaguely defined to include 'corporations and corporatism'.[49]

But the implications for digital television remain profound. The thirst for an opinion, almost as a 'style accessory', means that digital television almost *had* to come along in order to give a wide enough spread of opinions to satisfy the young:

There is a desire for an opinion. So we give brands a point of view. People have a thirst for a point of view. They look to that media to give them that. When they want to talk about the football manager's choice of the England team, they go to their football magazine. It gives them a point of view and makes them feel better about themselves. It's lazy. Opinions separate you from the run-of-the-mill. It helps the young if the media they are using help them to have opinions. What we've known for the last fifteen years is that people, from a political perspective, are becoming issue-focused rather than party-focused. You'll have someone who is up in arms about the shoddy way asylum seekers are treated, but that doesn't mean they are a socialist.

The great thing about digital TV for these people is that you can find the channel that has been specifically designed with your interests in mind – even scheduled with your lifestyle in mind. Programmes are now scheduled around the lifestyles of particular groups, and schedulers only put expensive programmes on when they know they're back from the pub. So successful digital channel operators give you a really interesting point of view about the world.

All of this poses big challenges for both advertisers and programme makers trying to determine what the young would like to see. If the young have no fixed opinions, are easily led and are desperate for a point of view, how do you create programming for them?

The youth market are very difficult to research because what they say is often very different to what they actually believe. Often what they believe is different to how they actually act. You must go on a shopping trip or a night out with them. Rather than get them to sit in a room in Crouch End with their mates and tell you about it, you get them to do it at first hand. What you find is that they will tell you which night clubs they go to and what they buy – then you go with them and they pick up a handful of flyers and they won't even realise that they've done it, or that their opinions come from those flyers. They wouldn't have told you that in a conventional research group.

You can ask someone 'Do you choose the brands you consume?' but the reality is often someone else chooses them for them. They will express an opinion when asked by someone they feel they must give a correct response to. One of the phrases we use is '*Strong opinions lightly held*'. The young are open to a tremendous amount of influence by people around them and by society. Now we talk about consumer ambush. We are becoming more concerned about the intrusive nature of advertising messages on peoples' lives. The problem with any form of intrusion is that you lose respect for the brand that is trying to do it. So you mustn't push your message – you must get consumers to pull you in. We see a great future in education channels, as they want to be taken on a journey which gives them opinions.

The important notion here is that the young will want to feel that they have selected a programme or a channel; they won't want to have a channel pushed in front of them. This undermines one of the first laws of advertising, and indeed of television promotion, which states that 'in order to give someone a message you first of all have to attract their attention'. However, it would appear that with the next generation this avenue is neither necessary nor admissible. Best to use other tactics to get their attention – for example, 'brand ambassadors':

The importance of other people influencing behaviour can never be underplayed. One of the interesting tactics is the use of brand ambassadors. There are a lot of companies that are actually paying people to be opinion formers and to create a sense of interest around a brand. We all know people who seem to have amazing influence in our social circle. The trick is to identify them and make them your brand ambassadors. Budweiser will pay what they call 'campus managers' on a Friday night to go into a bar and say 'I'll get the beers in – it's a Bud all round'. Everyone's quite happy with that – as you can imagine. Before you know, the next person is going to get a round by saying 'same again'. What's happening is that you're using the opinion of someone you are interested in. To do this successfully with the youth market, it is critical that it doesn't feel contrived.

The other tactic which we've used a lot here is to say: 'This is what represents the establishment. Why be part of that? Why not go your own way? You're an individual. You're brilliant – let's celebrate that. Be part of your community, dress the same, talk the same.' The reality is that the young do dress very much the same; they probably *are* the same – but they believe that they are in a small group of people.

The multiple, and often extraordinary, tactics being used by advertisers to influence the young are simply an advanced warning of
how difficult it will be to create anything approaching hit channels
or hot shows using traditional television thinking. Speaking to the
young now means being part of their community and giving them
a set of opinions of which they are proud – but which they might
switch for another set next week.

It means a television world of multiplicity, variety and many
links to different media. Only in that way can the communities and
the minds of the next generation of television viewers be reached.

The Commercial Breaks

EROSION

The old monopoly model of commercial television could sustain itself on just one source of income: advertising. In the States, for years the networks fought a fierce battle over audience 'share' – the percentage of all viewers who were watching a channel. This was important because television advertising was sold by the number of eyeballs – in other words, the number of people who had seen your advert. Advertisers didn't care about how the adverts were placed in relation to the programmes on the channel. Adverts were placed in a schedule until they reached the cumulative total of 'eyeballs' which an advertiser's campaign had bought. If audiences fell short of expectations, more slots were allocated to an advert until the shortfall was made up.

Sales houses later got more sophisticated: but not much. They began to charge a premium for being guaranteed a slot within a particular programme. But sales forces have remained wedded to pure numbers, even into the era of digital transmission. Jim Hytner, Marketing Director of ITV in the UK, puts it bluntly:

> Terrestrial sales forces have been trained to concentrate on selling the numbers and they tend not to sell the programmes. In many instances they tend not to watch the programmes either.

In Europe the position was more complicated, as the existence of publicly funded networks meant that advertising space was scarcer than it was in the United States. This had the peculiar effect of actually driving up the price of advertising on commercial television when the publicly funded networks gain more share. This is because advertisers had to buy more time on commercial networks to reach the same number of eyeballs – and were usually prepared to do so. So advertising on television remained essentially a 'number of eyeballs' game.

Multichannel television did not alter this model significantly. Advertising 'planners' – the people who book space on media – continued to pursue the largest number of eyeballs using the most expensive route: the main networks. But the old television-advertising model has started to show signs of fatigue with the arrival of digital television. The main reason for this is the sheer increase in channels available over digital, cable and satellite.

Figure 7.1 shows the relationship between the decline in viewing of a main network channel and the rise in viewing of channels which can only be received over cable and satellite. The main channel featured is the UK's ITV. The UK has been used as an example as the UK has the highest digital television penetration in the world – 40 per cent of households are able to receive it – and this trend is clearest in the UK.

What it spells out is the rapid decline of the main networks' share. Since 1994, ITV's share of the total UK audience has declined from 40 per cent to 25 per cent. Most advertising campaigns spend about 60 per cent of their budgets on television advertising and space. Lazily, they used to invest much of it in space on ITV. But, with ITV now reaching only half its old audience, where do they go to now?

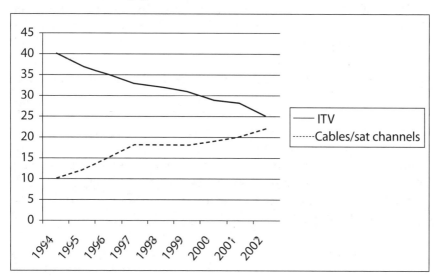

Figure 7.1. Decline in share of a commercial network channel compared with rise of digital channels[50]

It is also worth noting that the world's advertising industry, at the time of writing, has suffered a catastrophic decline in advertising spend. Some argue that ITV, and other networks like it, will revive when advertising spending revives – and it will then be exactly like the good old days.

This view is wrong. The changes wrought by digital television, both on the way in which audiences use television and the way in which advertisers are obliged to grab their attention, are far reaching and permanent. This is the beginning of a new kind of television and a new kind of advertising. In both worlds it is causing stresses and strains, as the new ways of thinking struggle to take over from traditions which are long established and moribund.

GRABBING NICHE EYEBALLS

Digital television fragments TV audiences. This is a big problem for the network channels as it erodes their share of the mass audience. However, it also opens up tremendous opportunities for advertisers. Digital offers for the first time the opportunity to cherry-pick segments of audiences and arrange them in a bouquet which reflects the audience the advertiser is trying to reach. But the problem is that advertising agencies have traditionally been reluctant to do this. Simon Guild, Chief Operating Officer of MTV Networks Europe, puts it like this:

> The structure of the advertising business means that most media buying deals are percentage deals. If you charge 10 per cent of how much is spent on a campaign, and the client comes through with £1m, you are going to make 10 per cent: in other words £100,000. Now if you make one deal with ITV, that's one piece of administration. But if you have to make fifteen deals with different satellite companies there's clearly a lot more involved. That may be a sceptical view. I'm not in the media planning business.

Although Guild describes himself as 'sceptical', this is a widely held explanation for why advertisers has been slow to embrace new ways of reaching niche audiences using digital television – it is too fiddly and expensive for them. Put simply, too many deals.

Why not do one deal with ITV? However, this is clearly not now in the client's interest, which is to reach as many relevant eyeballs as possible.

Rupert Miles was a publisher of magazines and then set up several commercial online ventures, including the interactive division of Carlton Television. He has watched the advertising industry's discomfort as digital television has proliferated:

> With the decline in share of ITV you now have to get more involved with more media owners in order to get the effective response that you desire. I think the agency world is going to have to invest in expertise and specialisation, and it's going to have to look at its cost base to see how it is going to cope.

Miles also believes that agencies now don't make anything like the 21 per cent of campaign spend which Saatchi and Saatchi was reputed to make in its early days:

> As an agency I will probably have negotiated a fee for the handling of the business and a small percentage commission on the media spend, and I will probably have agreed in advance with the client a production fee related to the treatment. When you look at the tens of millions of pounds going into a campaign a very low percentage actually sticks in the agency.

Again, this is a huge disincentive to innovate by buying small chunks of time on lots of digital television channels. That means that agencies, despite their declining share, still stick to buying time on the major networks. But there is a simple and compelling argument for buying space on a lot of niche channels: it is more efficient from the point of view of the client who is spending the advertising dollars:

> Advertising on niche television is more effective because, like MTV, it's got less wastage. When you go out with a big network campaign you pick up everybody, and you pay for everybody. When you go for MTV, or into children's television or another satellite TV area which is targeted at a specific audience, there is much more efficiency. So when you're buying ten thousand MTV viewers, or a hundred thousand or whatever it is, you really hit your audience.

That, put simply, is MTV's case that something has to change, and fast, in television advertising. Digital television is now a medium which is far more targeted and efficient than monopoly commercial television, and yet the agencies are reluctant to use digital television in an effective way.

So what are the agencies doing? Rupert Howell created HHCL, which in 2000 was named 'Agency of the Decade'[51] for its innovative approach to advertising over that entire period. He thinks that MTV's analysis is self-interested:

> MTV would say that because they think that they're not getting their fair share. 'Everybody trying to reach anyone under 25 should be spending their money on MTV', they would say. It's certainly not true. There's an awful lot of work which is done using specialist channels to reach specialist target audiences. Yet it is still true that the most cost-effective way of promoting mass market brands – brands that appeal across demographics and age groups – is mass advertising. But you can only do it as long as you capture the consumers' imaginations and engage with them. I think the real challenge of the multi-channel environment is that it puts such a massive premium on creativity. I think that where there are failures in campaigns on digital television it is because the creativity hasn't been up to the mark – or the people who are buying the creativity aren't prepared to take the kind of risks needed to achieve success.'

BRANDING CONTENT

The biggest impact of multichannel television on advertising has been a fundamental shift in the definition of advertising. This revolution is spreading from agencies like HHCL into the mainstream of advertising. However, its spread is by no means instantaneous. This is creating tension and frustration among providers of multiple packages of digital channels like MTV.

Branding content involves looking very carefully at the supply chain which goes into the creation of advertising messages. Rather in the way in which digital has uncovered unconsidered parts of the television supply chain, the same process has been set in train in advertising.

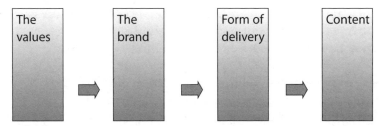

Figure 7.2. The process of producing new digital campaigns

Originally advertising concentrated on messages. Television was perfect for this as the messages could be scripted, shot and transmitted. They could then be placed on mass audience channels. But mass messages are only really effective in two circumstances:

■ When the entire audience is prepared to receive it in the same form
■ When competition for people's time and attention is limited.

These were precisely the circumstances of twenty years ago. There were few television channels, and relatively few other media apart from radio and print. In addition, audiences mainly came to television as a shared experience and tended to receive it as a family group.

All that has now flown out of the window (Chapter 2). Innovative advertisers are now wrestling urgently with the problem of how you reach the digital audience – more accurately, 'how you reach the audience in the digital age', as the needs of that audience have driven the growth of digital and not the other way around. Technology has no needs – it is passive until adopted by users.

There are several characteristics of the audience in the age of digital:

■ Their time is limited – as many media and experiences compete for their attention.
■ They are perfectly happy flicking between media – dabbling promiscuously. Somehow, they have also developed the knack of taking in information without being drawn in by its carrier. So they channel-hop and also hop between different modes of receiving information.

- They have a low tolerance of any very obvious message. In other words, conventional advertising doesn't work on them. They have to be seduced into watching.

These changes in the television audience, and particularly in its younger sections, are an appalling development for the advertising industry. Putting two women in a kitchen to praise the efficacy of a floor cleaner will no longer shift product. Even subtle variations – like having a man do it – are simply going to bounce off the digital audience.

Therefore, some advertisers have gone back to basics. Rather than coming up with a scripted message, they have started to debate the feelings and values which an advertiser is trying to engender in an audience. This is not new in advertising – but the way in which it is now being implemented is new.

Figure 7.2 shows the process of producing a campaign for a cocktail of digital media. The reason for creating 'cocktails' is that it is pointless exploiting just one medium: the new audience is not going to succumb to a single message repeated endlessly on one medium. They will only take notice of something which comes from *someone or something they trust, on a medium which they know is theirs*.

The most effective form of advertising is word-of-mouth from someone you know and like. In the past this was very difficult to orchestrate. However, the effect of digital technology has been to give this audience its own media, received by only its friends. This comes in two forms:

- Media which are so segmented that only you and your friends watch it (for example, the more exotic channel variations of MTV)
- Media which you and your friends have created yourselves.

As unlikely as this second category sounds, it is easy to engineer using digital technology. For example, many thirteen-year-olds now have their own chat rooms on the Internet which are only accessed by themselves and their friends. The group decides who are 'friends' and who to let in. This represents powerful bonding. Representing endless conversation at any time of the day and night, looked at in another way it is an electronic medium with one of the most focused audiences possible: only people who know you.

Editorially, if it were a publication, it would also have the most compelling content imaginable: only things about people you know. It is the ultimate medium.

Ultimately this is the direction in which advertising will migrate – moving the packaging of messages to media in which you and a group of trusted friends are the only participants. Broadcast technology could not hope to create this – but digital technology can, because of its ability to create networks which are specific to you.

In effect, what will happen in advertising is that two circles will increasingly overlap (Figure 7.3). These are the circle of the target audience for the product, and the circle of your community. Over the next twenty years much time and effort will be devoted to this by advertisers. It will take much perfecting – but the technology now exists to make it possible.

The ideal situation is when your community comes to believe that the product or service advertised is perfectly suited to its needs and desires. As the suggestion that this is so will be relayed by members of your community to other members, it is the ultimate form of viral targeting: targeting using an *unsuspecting host as the carrier*.

In order to move closer to the viral model, advertising is abandoning simple mass messages. To create an effective viral campaign the advertiser now has to work on the assumption that many new media must be provided with many different versions of content. This is because communities of young people flick between media – and in order to catch them it is necessary to inhabit several of the new media they might trust. But simple messages often don't translate over different media. For example

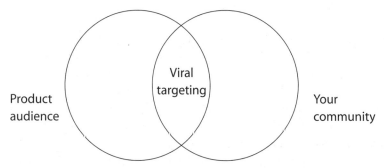

Figure 7.3. Getting your community to coincide with the product's target audience

the 'discussion in the kitchen' format, which works in television advertising, is impossible to translate to text messaging.

So advertisers are coming up with objects which embody the values they are trying to associate with a product. These objects can then be translated into several new media. So, as in Figure 7.2, the values go towards defining a brand which is embodied as an object present across several different media – and which then becomes the content, but in very many unrelated forms. These forms of campaign have the added advantage that their impact is very much larger than the campaign spend implies (if the spend is assessed using the old advertising model).

Ironically, one of the best recent examples of this is a campaign done for the troubled terrestrial digital platform ITV Digital, which is now in administration. As they were haemorrhaging cash and wanted to re-brand their platform, they needed an inexpensive way of getting into the consciousnesses of a lot of target audiences across many media.

So they tried to come up with some 'content' in the form of a 'branded object'. They wanted something that was friendly, laddish (as the appeal of ITV Digital was meant to be its rights to football league matches) and attractive to the young. They came up with an odd object – a woolly toy monkey. In the adverts he inhabited a house with a television couch potato, with whom he exchanged laddish repartee. But he also was given away free in shops, and he had his own chat show and inhabited the Internet. All this was at a fraction of the cost of a conventional campaign.

Rupert Howell says this is part of a trend where it is possible, because of the fragmentation of media and viewing, to enter the consciousness of an audience with far fewer television eyeballs than was previously possible:

It is a lot harder now to pick out the mass audiences but there is also a counter-balancing trend, which is that it takes a lot less money to enter the public consciousness. When I started out in the advertising business the sages of advertising, Proctor and Gamble, had worked out exactly the minimum level of advertising ratings at which you could afford to run a campaign in order to reach a mass audience and enter the consciousness of the house-wife. It was 100 ratings a week, in other words 400 ratings a month. Today Proctor and Gamble will tell you that you need 50 ratings a week – that is 200 ratings a month. Now a cynic would say that they have just lowered their expectations. What happens now is that advertising, if it touches a nerve, can enter mass consciousness at a much lower spend level than it could twenty years ago. So that's the equal and opposite force. If you look at graphs, like the one of ITV's decline, you would say that it's impossible to reach a mass audience. Yet people do. They do it by spreading the advertising around a number of channels. They pick up the opinion formers, primarily journalists – so you run everything on Sky News or CNN, because that runs in all the newsrooms around the world. The journalists then write about the advertising. Even in a multichannel environment it is possible to do mass advertising, although on paper it does not look feasible. There is a big but – you can't do it any more by bludgeoning people into submission. You have to do it by engagement with your brand. What you could do twenty years ago, but you can't do anymore, is what I call the Chinese water torture approach to advertising – where you saturate the media with advertising and eventually the viewer waves the white flag and says 'if you promise to stop showing this I will go and buy your product'. To do that now would cost so many millions you couldn't afford it. But if you do it at a lower level and catch the zeitgeist you can be very successful.

So while the hold of the main network channels declines an equal and opposite tendency is developing: the ability to penetrate mass consciousness through many sources. This is a function of the sheer ubiquity of niche media, which allow many ways into mass consciousness. However, fewer people now have shared electronic experiences. So the advertising industry is now grappling with trying to use advertising to influence those who influence the mass mind.

Successful future uses of digital technology will develop this approach and make it more sophisticated.

WHEN IS CONTENT 'COOL'?

The idea of 'niche penetration', and the use of branded objects across many media, is useless unless the target audience embraces the basic content. To the 16–24 year olds this means asking whether it is 'cool'. Yahoo, in its earliest form in Sunnyvale,

California, used to employ web searchers to look at new web sites and decide whether they were 'cool'. If they were, they got linked to Yahoo. Now every young person does this for himself or herself, consciously or unconsciously, as they encounter electronic media.

As ridiculous as this all may seem, it is of critical importance for the likes of MTV. Simon Guild says:

> Last year we did a thing called 'Sources of Cool', which considers where 'cool' comes from. We asked: 'Where do people get cool?' If it can be obtained from somewhere, then where? So we went to different countries around Europe and we asked people about how they dress, where they got fashion from, where their reference point instincts come from. That research enabled us to find out. We've also used that with a lot of our advertisers to help them understand where these kids are going.

Of most concern to Simon Guild, and to the management of other digital channels, is a gruesome implication of the 'targeting the mass through many media' strategy – which is that the same advert is useless across many media. For example, if a network advert is simply played out on MTV it won't be relevant to their 'cool' audience:

> Many years ago we were looking at detergent and advertising and we asked people 'do you think soap powder could appear on MTV?' and everyone said 'No'. So we showed them a soap powder ad, which featured a pop band and stonewashed jeans and whatever it was, and they went 'oh, that's great'. It was all in the execution. They would accept anything as long as the execution was relevant.

MTV have become so frustrated with the advertising industry producing adverts which are not 'cool' enough for their audience that they have taken the law into their own hands:

> We do make some ads. We made one for the Euro actually. It's a very small ad. Basically it features these guys doing hand movements – they had to audition an awful lot of people – and then they finish up with the sign of the Euro. It's cool how they use their fingers to do the Euro symbol. That's quite a smart ad.

We do it really because sometimes clients comes to us and say 'we need to get on air, can you do something for us, our agency won't or can't', and it tends to be more about being a last resort. Actually, we've made some great stuff. But it's a specific thing: we don't want to be on the hook for the success of the advertising that runs on our channel, otherwise we're in a very different game which advertising agencies do better than we do. So we do it as a last resort.

However, it is a terrible indictment of the present state of the advertising industry that clients are forced into even considering having the management of the television channel make them an advert. Even if the circumstances were that the client was too mean to pay agency rates, it seems that something is severely wrong with an industry which can't produce different kinds of content for different niche channels at an affordable price. Rupert Howell sees the problem differently:

We're living in a world where pressure is being put on agency fees, and on production budgets, all in the name of providing more money for the live part of advertising, which is the media spend. The truth of the matter is that all our media spend is a total waste of money unless you have great ideas and produce them in a way which is appropriate: not necessarily expensive, but appropriate for the medium in which they are running. I worked with MTV twelve years ago – doing their advertising – and they were saying the same thing then. So nothing has changed in that sense because of the media environment. I think the issue is much more about 'do we have the creative firepower to cut through in this media environment?' Have we got brave enough clients who say, if we're going to aim at this target group on MTV and at their grandparents at the same time (perhaps the product would be children's savings bonds) we do something different for the mainstream channels. There are certainly not many financial directors who would sign off on doubling the production spend in order to make more efficient use of the media.

Eric Salama, from his seat on the board of the world's largest advertising agency, WPP, also sees this problem, but views it as a general malaise which always develops when there are many new media developing:

I think that there are certain platforms where we haven't figured out what advertising should really look like. People talk about online advertising a lot, and why hasn't it taken off more. I think a fundamental reason for this is that no-one has yet created effective content for online.

If you think about other media, you could argue that when TV first developed the content was radio content that people took to TV. It took TV a while to figure out what was unique about TV and therefore what content it required. I think that every media requires content that is appropriate to it. The same with advertising. We haven't really figured out yet what form of advertising is suited to Playstations, and what form is suited to online. I think we've worked it out for print, and for magazines and TV, but now there are new media. So I think from that point of view there is a challenge – not just from the advertising but from the content point of view – as to whether it is pure content or advertising content, figuring out what type of content is relevant to some of the new media.

Why isn't more work being done on content which is appropriate to new media, like digital television? The questions here seem to be twofold:

- Are clients prepared to take risks with content, running different forms of advertising across different media?
- Does the structure of the advertising industry itself work against innovation in advertising?

This second point is subtle but important. The advertising industry has for years been divided between creative production agencies, who design and make the advertisements, and the media buyers who purchase the space across the many media in which a campaign might run. However, new media like digital television make a nonsense of this distinction, because they demand that decisions about content and about the media on which they run be made inseparable. It isn't simply a question of producing an advertisement which runs across all media. Rupert Howell sees this as a critical stumbling block:

The problem is exacerbated by the split between creative agencies and media buying agencies. The creative agencies now argue, in a bit of a vacuum, that creativity is paramount (and they *would* say that, wouldn't they?); and the media agencies argue, also in a vacuum, that media selection, cleverness and buying is paramount (and they *would* say that, wouldn't they?). The concern is that this has driven a wedge between the two. What you don't get is someone saying that you need a holistic view – that the magic actually comes from a combination of great creativity, well produced, intelligently placed, and cost-efficiently bought. That's where the great relationships used to be – and they've been split asunder by the divide between creativity and media. People in both media and creative agencies are very concerned about this.

What's happened is that the vacuum has been filled by a new kind of agency, originally typified by Michaeledes and Bednash, and most notably by Naked. Once the agency comes up with the idea – the object – Naked comes up with all the other ideas about how you could use it. For example, with the ITV Digital monkey they came up with making a star who could be interviewed by magazines, giving it a show for kids. They filled that gap in the middle. This new kind of agency has emerged, and I think that that proves there's a need for it.

The advertising industry is trying to give birth to new structures and ideas which will deal with the immediate problem that the network channels are disappearing fast. An inability to tell clients how to reach mass audiences will severely limit growth.

Difficulties that are more profound lie in creating content for diverse and fragmented audiences – which is the obvious impact of digital television. In order to achieve this the advertising industry will have to look not only into its own structure, but also at its power to persuade clients that the future lies in multiple advertising, not in endlessly repeating the same material across six hundred channels.

THE FUTURE OF TELEVISION ADVERTISING

The biggest impact of digital television industry on advertising will be to diminish the importance of the thirty-second television advertisement. These mini-feature films have achieved an almost iconographic status in the industry, helped by generous hype attached to the adverts themselves. But, in an age where no single channel can reach more than a quarter of the television audience (and even this share is falling), this form of advertising is on its way out.

What are likely to replace it are multiple adverts: pieces of content which extend the message of the client's brand. Rupert Howell says that it is often difficult persuading clients to commission multiple pieces of content. On digital television space is cheaper, however, and digital production techniques have massively lowered the costs of production. In the days of monopoly TV it would not have been possible to take something which was nakedly linked to an advert and have it present a children's programme. But regulators do not apply stringent rules to channels watched by only 0.5 per cent of the television audience.

In this way the advertising industry will become more about 'branded content' than making television adverts which cost millions of dollars. However the problem with this, for the industry itself, is that its fees will reduce with the lowering of the campaign spend. It follows that advertising agencies will have to find another way of charging for their services: for example, by retainer (which is what HHCL has been doing for many years).

More profound is the need to re-organise the way in which the industry is organised – particularly addressing the split between media buyers and the creative agencies that make the adverts. The split came about partly because clients felt they got better value for money if they separated the two. However, if it can be demonstrated that clients can reach a bigger audience more potently by combining media buying and creative agencies then it will happen.

The cyclical downturn in the industry has left clients more inquisitive about evaluating the potency of campaigns. Now they would like ways of measuring the effectiveness of a campaign. This issue is dealt with in the next Chapter. But digital television is far better at this than old analogue television could ever have hoped to be. Clients seeing the results of these evaluations, showing the efficacy of choosing media and content as one seamless operation, will push change faster in the industry than visionary statements from industry leaders. So the pace of change relies on how well the digital platforms and channels market information about their subscribers' response to new digital campaigns.

That creates the very real possibility that MTV's involvement in making its own adverts was not a passing phase, but the start of a structural shift in the industry towards television channels branding content for product owners. After all, if a digital channel is to succeed it must understand intimately how to brand its own content to give itself an appealing identity.

In the end, a portion of advertising spending may be slipping from the advertising industry's grasp into the hands of the channel owners. In the age of digital, channel owners can no longer rely on advertisers simply buying media space. Other sources of income need to be developed and guarded jealously.

Finding Business Models That Work

IN THE BOX

All of the interviewees quoted in this book agree that digital technology radically changes the way in which broadcasters will make money. No television business model is sacrosanct anymore. Digital television allows newcomers into television, and new ways of making money out of the television viewer. However, television broadcasters are not *guaranteed* to make money (as used to be the case in the days of monopoly terrestrial television). In Europe, where digital transmission is highly developed, there are almost as many new business models as there are channels.

It is early days. However, it is already possible to talk about successful digital television business models. The converse is equally true – there are many unsuccessful ones as well. In the UK alone the following digital channels, most of them less than two years old, folded in 2001:

- Channel East
- Wellbeing
- Whereits.at
- Rapture
- The Automotive Channel
- (.tv)
- The Money Channel
- Simply Money
- Taste
- Scene One.[52]

Many of these channels made a simple mistake. They assumed that if they got their subject matter right they would prosper under the plain vanilla, multi-channel model of taking some subscription

....

130

income and selling some advertising. This is about as wrong as you can be in digital television. Setting up a digital television channel involves answering two fundamental questions:

- Can you find an audience which is underserved?
- How do you get income from them?

In answering the second question, all assumptions should be jettisoned. Everything should be questioned and regarded as up for grabs.

Finding answers to *how* and *why* a digital channel works may involve new and unfamiliar routes. In digital, always think 'outside the box' before you climb into a box someone else created. Someone else's business model will almost certainly be best exploited by them, and give you no room for growth.

OUT OF THE BOX

To illustrate how business models can vary in digital TV, Table 8.1 illustrates the models behind three separate channels available on European digital systems. By any measure of new media business they are all successful, as they all make a profit. However, their

	ITV	*The Box*	*Shop America*
Programme acquisition costs	High – need to create high quality entertainment	Low (most material free from pop industry)	Low (presenters in a studio with product)
Revenue streams	Advertising	Majority of income from premium call lines	■ Premium call lines ■ Commission from goods sold
Audience profile	Mass audience channel slightly skewed to females	Teens who have access to phones	Self-improvement fanatics

Table 8.1. Different business models in digital television

business models are all radically different. Only one (that of ITV) has the conventional structure of an old terrestrial network.

ITV has high programme acquisition costs, as it needs to hang onto a mass audience who are tuning in to see something new and entertaining and this means it has to spend big money to get the right material. Mass audiences are very critical of content, and demand the latest talent and their sporting events live. But as ITV is also on the terrestrial broadcasting system it has a very high reach in the UK (although it cannot be seen outside it). This allows it to derive the great majority of its income from television advertising if it can hang onto a large enough audience. Media buyers tend to use it as one-stop shop for clients who want promotion for their products.

The Box is very different. It plays pop videos and offers viewers the chance to choose the next record by dialling in through a premium call line. Premium call lines often charge a dollar a minute for use of a service – with most of the revenue going to The Box. The Box derives most of its income from these premium lines. The television channel is, in effect, used as a lure to get teenagers to use a premium cost call line. Its audience is therefore teenagers with access to a phone – and not necessarily one for which they pay the bill.

More bizarre is Shop America. Richard Brooke, the former Finance Director of BSkyB, describes it in this way:

> Shop America only sells five products:
> - How to improve your memory.
> - How to do mental arithmetic.
> - How to improve your golf swing.
> - How to flatten your tummy.
> - And it also sells a frying pan that doesn't need oil.
>
> They have never changed their programming. They have been on the air for two years. And they continue to sell large amounts of merchandise.

Shop America works on yet another model – that of an e-commerce operation which happens to be on television. Unlike other television shopping channels it has a very restricted product range – but this massively simplifies stock control and distribution. It also gives the channel advantages with programme content, as it needs very little illustrative material to talk about its products. Shop

America ran a risk that there would be no audience (or rather 'buyers') for this service – but there are, and it works. It is a model which no old-fashioned public service broadcaster would or could ever contemplate. Television has changed beyond recognition.

Richard Brooke watches all this with wry amusement. After getting BSkyB to profitability as its Finance Director he took on the visionary challenge of creating an alternative television platform to Sky – but one which existed as a virtual platform within the Sky platform. This was to make use of a piece of European Union legislation which allows anyone with the money to take space on a digital satellite platform, and protects them from prohibitive rental fees. He is almost certainly the first person in the world to lead a team to create a television platform within a platform. His company which did this, DVC, is no longer trading. Despite trying and not quite succeeding, he enjoys the variety of business models which digital television creates:

> I think the real impact of digital television has been to move the television model from one of franchising to one of publishing. Before multichannel television came along you had a very small number of channels because bandwidth wasn't available. What bandwidth was available was basically owned or franchised by the government. What multichannel television started, and what digital television has really completed, is a change of that model into one of publishing. Now it's no longer bandwidth which determines whether you run a channel or not: it's the economic viability of that channel. Television is now the same as magazines. On one hand you have Conde Nast, who run extraordinarily profitable glossy magazines which turn over hundreds of millions of dollars; at the other extreme you have *Caravanning Monthly* – which appeals to a tiny minority who are also prepared to pay good money for it. And digital television is like that now.

WORKING MODELS

A very simple rule in a publishing environment is that success depends on how well you play the particular game in which you participate. Television executives find this difficult to understand as they are all so programmed to competing in a straight fight for ratings. Unfortunately the advertising industry – which should know better – also finds it very difficult to comprehend that there may now be many different games being played by television operators. This, of course, implies different sources of revenue and so different kinds of advertising.

There are now at least twelve distinct business models in use in the digital television market. They are:

1. Platform
2. Total vertical integration
3. Channel management (or 'content branding')
4. Rights to hits
5. Old terrestrial network
6. Low rights costs: plus globalisation
7. Low rights costs: broadcast locally
8. High rights costs: plus globalisation
9. Low rights costs: allied with selling
10. High rights costs: allied with selling
11. A platform within a platform
12. Interactivity

Some are proven successes; on others the jury is out. Others are possible but are not actually in use (normally because even on paper they don't work out).

Taking each in turn here is a guide to where they are being used – and whether or not they are future winners.

1. Platform

Platforms are so fundamental to digital television that Chapter 4 was devoted to them. They have uncovered the essential and critical link with the viewer – allowing a direct relationship with them in much the same way that any subscription service is able to know and anticipate the tastes of its customer base.

But how well do they work as a business model? To be a successful platform operator you need to have:

- Channels and content which people are prepared to pay for.
- Feisty and determined marketing to make sure potential subscribers are aware of you.
- Encryption technology which cannot be broken by hackers – this is essential as you are operating a gateway to content which you are giving people permission to view.

- The means of growing the service fast – otherwise your backers may refuse to cover your losses in the early years.
- A reliable customer support centre which is able to field everything, from enquiries from potential subscribers to queries about technical problems.
- Satellite, cable or terrestrial distribution – which may or may not involve expensive acquisitions and licensing.

This is an expensive game, which only people with deep pockets can play. There are plenty of platforms which, although not insolvent, have recently stared down that abyss. For example, the pan-European digital cable network UPC got into difficulty with its cash flow, and has been picked up for a song by John Malone's Liberty Media Group. Malone is now circling the cash-strapped NTL in the UK.

In the UK the digital terrestrial platform, ITV Digital, has burnt £1 billion of its investors' money and is in administration. Carlton, one of the owners, reportedly wants to ditch it to allow Carlton to be taken over by German media giant Bertelsmann. As the Chinese say, opportunity and crisis are the same thing – particularly if the victim is left holding a digital television platform which is under performing.

There are other easy mistakes to make with platforms. BSkyB in the UK was forced to give in to moves by the BBC to ensure that they could have carriage on the Sky platform at prices which are 'fair, reasonable and non-discriminatory'. This ruling was then enshrined in EU legislation. In the States, digital satellite platform Echostar is facing similar strictures from the Federal Communications Commission. Echostar recently took two Disney-owned channels off its platform and discovered itself facing a Federal Judge who blocked the move.[53]

Almost the worst aspect of being a platform owner is the need to grow the subscriber base fast. In the UK this has meant giving away the equipment necessary to receive the service. It now seems likely that one of the prime reasons for the cash difficulties now being experienced by Kirch Gruppe's pay TV operations in Germany is that they failed to give away set top boxes – and so stunted their subscriber growth. Kirch Media is now saddled with 4.4 billion Euro of debt and is in administration.[54]

In conclusion, platforms on their own represent such a high-risk way to enter digital television that an entrepreneur would be ill-advised to start one up. Much better to wait for one to fail – and acquire it on the cheap, as John Malone of Liberty Media is doing.

2. Total vertical integration

It is easy to object to the above analysis in that Rupert Murdoch succeeded in starting his own platform, in the shape of BSkyB and AsiaNet. He has failed so far to acquire DirecTV in the US, but possibly it is just a matter of time before he gets the grand slam – giving him a global satellite platform.

However, the fact remains that he didn't use the simple 'platform' model to enter digital TV. He used *total vertical integration*. This means that Murdoch's vision was always to control both the content on his platform and the distribution. Creating a platform was only part of the equation.

Richard Brooke was on the team that got BSkyB from its early stages, where no other investors wanted to buy a stake in it, to a present capitalisation of £14.5 billion.[55] The business model was always very simple:

> What I can say is that those who control both the distribution and content are going to win. It's extraordinarily expensive to dominate both areas of distribution and content, but Sky has done extraordinarily well in the UK because it's been able to do that. Cable has struggled because it's never been able to get a hold on content. The UK experience has proved how dismal that has been for them.

This model, therefore, is only for those with the resources and the cunning of media owners. Brooke is very sceptical that anyone starting from outside a media business can ever come up with a winning combination both for creating content and for a digital distribution network. The publishing analogy is a good one as those who understand publishing, as Murdoch does, will probably be able to understand how to make a success of vertical integration: and how to cover the costs of such an expensive strategy.

3. Channel management (new digital channel start-ups)

Most entrepreneurs contemplating entering digital television look no further than starting a television channel which gets its revenue mainly from subscription and advertising. This is myopic. Looking down the list of the 26 digital channels planning to launch in the UK in the next year, it is impossible to see any but two which do not simply reproduce something which is already available – or has been available and which has failed. The two exceptions are:

- The Job Channel – employment services
- The Property Channel – property services.

These two are certainly niche. They may also have outstanding and interesting business models. For the sake of their shareholders, it would be nice if they did.

The problem with starting another national digital television channel based on subscription and advertising is that the model doesn't really work for channels with high content-acquisition costs. Channel 4 in the UK will continue to struggle with its new digital channel E4 because:

- It only has the rights to programming in the UK (the channel remains limited to the UK digital audience – so it cannot globalise).
- The programming it needs to create an audience is expensive (E4 screens first runs of US hits like *ER*).
- It is supported only by UK-based subscriptions and advertising.

Richard Brooke says of this model:

> The economics of running a digital channel are that you can operate one for about a million pounds a year. Advertising is the least likely model to succeed for a new digital channel. Take for example E4, which received much publicity for spending a vast amount of money on programming from Warner Brothers. This was not an advertising model entirely because they get a per-subscriber fee from Sky, who were very keen that E4 should be in the basic subscriber package. But it's still a very difficult model to work successfully because you do have to sell advertising. The per-subscriber fee isn't going to cover the operating costs. Relying heavily on advertising revenues in a digital start-up is impossible, really.

Channel 4 will argue that when advertising picks up all will be fine – but that depends heavily on whether you believe that advertising is undergoing a cyclical or a structural downturn. If the latter, E4 is doomed.

There are those who think that it is still worth trying to make a go of the channel model. Jim Hytner, Marketing Director of the ITV Network in the UK, thinks of channels as the primary tool for branding content, giving them a hugely enhanced value. He points out that ITV's current hit show *Pop Idol* was pitched in a pub, and ITV could have then chosen to put it on at 4 in the afternoon. However, they then put it on at prime time on a Saturday night. This, plus expensive production, gave it its value. In Hytner's view ITV could, and should, have taken a stake in the show:

> If you can develop brilliant channels, eventually you can maximise your revenues by exploiting the programme rights which you have within the channel. It's a great business model to say 'ITV – had we taken ownership of *Pop Idol* – had we said that we would take 50 per cent of the exploitation rights, we'd have paid a bit more for the show.' It's just a perfect model. We schedule it in a brilliant slot. It then takes off. You get the merchandise rights, the video rights. It's a great business to be in.

But this will not work for most channels, as they have neither the mass audience to create a mass phenomenon (like *Pop Idol*) nor the cash to do such an expensive show. The model Hytner is describing is only truly open to old terrestrial networks at the moment. And, as his example shows, they are not grabbing the opportunities.

Most traditional digital channel start-ups will fail unless they are very clear, and creative, about the source of their revenues.

4. Rights to hits

Higher up the television supply chain than the channels, the business model which works well is owning the rights to a hit programme or event. This is easier said than done. But it is the route to riches for independent production companies. The problem is that to create a hit, like *Who Wants To Be A Millionaire?*, independent producers need a fair amount of co-operation from channel or platform owners both in the placing of new series and in the amount invested in their promotion. *Millionaire* was touted

around for a couple of years unsuccessfully before an ITV sched-
uler was looking for a format to run on consecutive nights and
found the *Millionaire* proposal in a filing cabinet. Such a path to
success is not taught in business schools and is not for those of a
nervous disposition.

However there are some rights that the channels and the platforms simply cannot do without – and which the clever independents
wrap up as programmes. The three most common are:

- Sports rights.
- Talent rights.
- Character rights.

Sports rights are mainly held by teams or sports associations (like
FIFA) and are auctioned by those organisations. It is uncommon
for an independent producer to get hold of them – but there are
signs that this will be usual in the future. For example, Manches-
ter United has started its own football channel (and so is, in effect,
acting as an independent). Formula One, the motor racing event
company, also threatens to go it alone with its own channel from
time to time. There are also instances of individual sporting events,
like boxing, where the event is sold via pay per view. However as a
source of revenue for independents this is still in its infancy. It is
more likely that the sporting rights owners will declare themselves
to have an independent production operation and enter television
in that way.

This is certainly what has happened in the television talent
industry. Many comedians and performers first establish their
name on the screen and then insist that if a network wants any
more material featuring their skills it will have to commission
programmes from their independent production company. Usually
this works. The *Monty Python* team were one of the first groups of
performers to build this relationship with the television companies, as a result of which they still own the rights to most of the
shows.

Character rights are an extension of this method. It involves
creating and building characters, then making television
programmes around them. If the character brands are strong
enough this can be a powerful way of extracting money from channels or platform owners. Disney are the masters of this, and
usually use the cinema as the main means of character building.

However it is expensive – and an operator has to have supreme confidence in its branding and merchandising skills.

However it remains interesting how much better many independent producers are at creating hits than channels or platforms owners – which comes down to how good your organisation is at innovation. But innovation costs money. It is better for independent producers to get channels to pay for pilots than for channels to insist that the independent producer pays for the cost of the pilot. However that negotiation depends on how badly the channel wants the material.

5. Old terrestrial network (not globalised)

This model applies to almost any of the major networks: for example CBS, ABC, ITV in the UK, or RTL in France. These networks find it very expensive to globalise as their schedules rely on shows (often American in origin), or on non-international sports rights. This means that they have to survive as purely national phenomena. Most have reacted to the advent of digital by creating extra channels which extend their brand in some way. For example, ITV has created ITV 2 – which runs longer versions of existing shows and allows viewers to join in interactively with shows like *Who Wants To Be A Millionaire?*

There is a big debate about how well the old terrestrial networks will come through the onslaught of digital technology. Your position on it largely depends on what you think will happen to the old terrestrial channels' advertising revenues, which are their major source of revenue.

Richard Brooke sees a highly symbiotic relationship developing between the advertising agencies and the old commercial networks:

> Advertising agencies work best when you have a big advertiser here and a big television company there, and put the two together in a creative way. Critical mass will remain with the old television networks, and will remain a profitable thing to have. Being a network involves massive investment in programming – so the barriers to entry are very high. That's the good news for them. While they continue to rely on a critical mass of audience, they will have to invest large sums in programming just to get that audience. Content inflation has always been higher than

normal inflation – but it has always been sustained by higher-than-average advertising inflation. So you need the two to prop each other up. The model relies heavily on *advertising inflation.*

But 'advertising inflation' is a very awkward thing to rely on. Richard Brooke is assuming that the amounts the old networks can charge for advertising will continue to outstrip the rate of general inflation by a considerable margin. Several factors argue against this:

- The decline in total audience share of the major networks means that they will find it harder and harder to raise prices above inflation each year. The major networks, under attack from clever niche channels, will lose much of their ability to reach a mass audience.
- Other media, such as the Internet and electronic developments, will lure younger viewers away from television – and so result in it losing its pre-eminence with the next generation of eyeballs. Stripped of younger viewers, TV advertising rates will be hard to justify.
- Under pressure from their clients, advertisers will get smarter (as examined in Chapter 7). This means that agencies will buy space on a number of new media, and across a number of digital channels, in order to reach highly targeted audiences. The networks will lose out to this structural move.

In summary, there are several ways for networks to go but standing still is not an option. Caught in the headlights, ultimately digital technology and all its associated social changes will run them over.

6. Low rights costs: plus globalisation

This is the MTV model. They are superb at it. Very few transnational media businesses make any profits at all. But revenues in MTV Networks International increased 19 per cent to $600 million in 2001, while operating profits grew 50 per cent to $135 million.[56]

MTV learnt early that globalising a channel is not enough – viewers will always demand a local feel or the channel won't appeal to them. Worse, unless a channel talks to its audience advertisers won't use it. MTV's figures owe a lot to spotting these trends ahead of the pack and acting very fast.

The other critical element in MTV's model is the low cost of its rights. Pop videos come cheap. All MTV has to supply is local shows and presentation, and the occasional big global event which gives the feeling of exclusive access to the stars. Simon Guild, Chief Operating Officer of MTV Networks Europe, says:

> It's about star power; it's about networking; it's about being able to reach out to people wherever they are and touch them. We can bring stars to you because we interview them when they are in America or Japan, or elsewhere, and can put them on your screen. We have access – unique access.

It is a model in which you might expect competition, as the core content is easy to obtain. EMAP in the UK has introduced an alternative model in The Box. VIVA, owned by AOL Time Warner and Vivendi, is MTV's biggest rival in Europe but is currently reporting losses. However, MTV is attempting to raise barriers to entry through investment in the brand, which means invigorating the brand locally. It also means getting the political contacts and the clout to be allowed to transmit in large foreign markets. It is already present in India and China.

MTV now reaches 375 million households and is the biggest broadcaster on the planet. If you have the courage and determination, and the contacts, low-cost content on a global scale can work a treat – and is only really possible because of the economies of transmission offered by digital technology.

The trick is to find content which is as inexpensive as MTV's, and where the owners don't care about global transmission. This model only exists, after all, because another industry (the pop music industry) sees MTV as a useful means of promotion. There are currently only two other categories which begin to come near to pop music:

- Corporate videos: where companies are keen to bear production costs in order to get their message out.
- Consumer goods: where companies will supply video material in order to sell a product. This accounts for the low production costs of many shopping channels.

The first category appeals to such a niche audience that no-one has really succeeded in making a business channel profitable.

The second has led to many shopping channels: the most success-ful global brand is QVC, which works on a similar business model to MTV's. At the moment MTV doesn't really do selling – but in time it might. It is a logical extension of its business model.

The main risk that MTV runs is that the pop music industry might decide to charge for the rights to show its output. In MTV's favour is the fact that the pop industry is highly fragmented, and would find it hard to agree such a strategy – and that it is in a managerial mess. However, the pop industry did act together to stop songs being given away for free in its court case against Internet song distribution site Napster. There are also signs that the music industry, after years of excess and indisci-pline, is cleaning up its act. It is certainly ironic that while the music industry spends a lot of money protecting the copyright of its audio products it still gives broadcasters its videos at well below cost.

7. Low rights costs: broadcast locally

This is a very efficient way to make money out of digital TV if there is a very distinct and underserved niche audience present in a national market. The proposition works by obtaining rights which are cheap in that market but of intense interest to a particular group. Richard Brooke ran several of these channels for his DVC service. These included several Hindu film channels – and he bought the content direct from Bollywood for showing in the UK:

> You can actually acquire valuable programming which is at cheap rates because it's not in its major market. The same programming, were you to acquire it in India, would cost you a fortune. Once it's out of its territory it stops being premium programming.

Brooke put these up as premium subscription channels – in other words, you pay a fee in addition to the basic fee charged by the plat-form in order to receive them. Since an Indian film channel is of intense interest to that community, and because that community is affluent, the business model works.

It is unlikely that there are an infinite number of such niches. However, in the UK at least, Brooke's niche is currently unfilled because the funding was pulled from his company.

8. High rights costs: plus globalisation

This is the model used by both the Disney channels and by CNN. They broadcast globally, with varying degrees of localisation, but their content is difficult and costly to produce.

Disney is an unusual example because its channels, in a way, are a marginal activity. Disney's core activity is producing major films (and highly profitable animations). However, it has decided that rather than sell them to third parties it will put them on a series of localised channels across the world. It also produces a lot of made-for-television material to feed its channels. In the UK there are now five channels, all segmented and appealing to different age groups (such as pre-school). The platform owners all fight to have Disney channels as part of their basic package. So, with the advent of digital, the more Disney-branded channels which Disney added the more revenue came in through subscription. This was because platform owners, keen to have Disney as part of their basic package, would still add a generous slug of subscription revenue for each additional channel. Such is the power of the Disney brand.

This is at the heart of Disney's strategy. Paul Robinson, Head of Programming for Disney channels, says:

> Our view is that any content we have should drive whatever platform we're putting the content on, and therefore there should be an upside both for us and the platform owner. The goal, to make the business work, is to have a shared agenda of mutual self-interest, and that self-interest is to drive the growth of the platform.

CNN has similar high production costs and also a potent brand. However, it has struggled with localisation – the costs of running bureaux in every territory in which it is transmitted would be prohibitive. This means that, despite anchoring its CNN International channel from a heady mixture of London, New York and Tokyo, it still tends to be the first choice of Americans stranded in foreign hotels. It is global – but does it appeal locally? It has also not been as successful as MTV at penetrating new territories. This is probably because the Chinese see pop music as marginally less threatening than uncensored Western news – so CNN International currently reaches an audience less than half the size of MTV's.

It would be hard to deny that this business model works. But it is a big advantage to have world-class material on which to build a global digital network. And basically that means being American. The only European content owner who has even approached this model is the UK's BBC, with a 'BBC America' channel in the States. But the BBC is very unusual, as it has a guaranteed income and can afford a risk profile entrepreneurs only dream about.

9. Low rights costs: allied with selling

Home shopping channels have provided an unexpectedly robust model for digital TV. Barry Diller kicked off the trend when he was fired from Murdoch's Fox TV and set up QVC, the home shopping channel. At the time he was described as mad. But QVC remains the home shopping market leader. The shopping model has much to recommend it:

- Low rights costs: as you only need a presenter in a studio with examples of the items for sale.
- Positive cash flow: as shoppers pay up front with their credit cards – faster than the channels are having to pay for the stock. This may seem unglamorous but it is why bankers get so excited about supermarkets and pubs – they generate heaps of up-front cash.
- The potential to make revenue from premium service phone lines which shoppers use to order the goods. But currently few shopping channels do this, instead using free lines to encourage shoppers to call.
- The ability to migrate seamlessly to some of the interactive facilities available on digital television – like interactive shopping.

Some shopping channels have tried to distinguish themselves by concentrating on specialised areas. For example, Wellbeing in the UK was a joint venture between Granada Television and Boots, a large chain of chemists. The thinking behind this was that an existing High Street brand would help establish the channel, but this venture closed early in 2002. Granada is also attempting to extract itself from its joint venture with Littlewoods, a home shopping catalogue company.[57]

However as the number of shopping channels grows inevitably there will be increasing specialisation, as that is the only way these channels will stay in business.

10. High rights costs: allied with selling

On the face of it this would appear an absurd proposition – why burden your channel with high rights costs when you only need a presenter in a studio to sell something?

The answer is that when you are selling something intangible, like a television programme or an event, it makes very good business sense. Viewers are only going to buy programmes which are difficult to obtain elsewhere, such as first run movies and special sporting events. Consequently, the costs to the rights to the programming, by definition, will not be cheap.

Selling 'intangible' material – like software, or rights to play games – via the interactive elements of the digital box is a small but growing area.

Most platforms in the start-up phase are only interested in two things: gaining more subscribers and reducing 'churn' (in other words, the rate at which those subscribers leave the service). However, when a digital television platform reaches maturity its management becomes far more concerned with 'ARPU' – Average Revenue Per Unit (in other words, the amount of money each subscribing household is paying to the platform). One essential component in driving up ARPU is increasing the amount households are spending on pay per view movies and events. Table 8.2 shows the amount of revenue BSkyB is projected to make (projection by Bank of America Securities) from each subscribing household for the years 2001–6, by type of revenue. These types are subscription revenue, revenue from pay per view, and revenue from the new source of interactive sales and games. There is a steady increase in the amount of money which will come from pay per view services for intangible product – rising to 14 per cent of revenue from households by 2006.

So Sky, as a platform, anticipates that pay per view activities will increase in importance as a source of revenue. But pay per view is a difficult market in which to participate. Any competitor needs movies and events for which people are prepared to pay extra. One of the reasons Sky can obtain such material is its formidable presence in the market, and the fact that it is bulk-buying movies from

	2001	2002	2003	2004	2005	2006
Basic subscription	270	293	308	321	335	350
Pay per view	15	17	20	24	27	29
Interactive revenues	3	10	17	22	25	28
Total revenues per household	288	320	345	367	387	407
Percentage of revenue from pay activities	6%	8%	11%	13%	13%	14%

Table 8.2. Projected income per household for BSkyB

the Hollywood studios all the time. It is doubtful that players with less clout can make this model work as successfully.

11. A platform within a platform

'Platforms within platforms' are a very new idea. For the time being they can only exist in Europe, because the EU has passed a directive requiring that the primary platform owner will not make their economics prohibitive.

A platform consists essentially of content, a delivery mechanism (which could be cable, satellite or terrestrial) and a subscriber management system (see Chapter 4). It is not possible to create a successful platform without expensive marketing – as building one is about obtaining subscribers as fast as possible. Marketing costs on the Sky platform alone in 2001 were £378 million.[58]

Platform owners, once they have achieved a critical mass of subscribers, are in a position of power. Channels want to be present on a successful platform in order to increase their audience (and so their advertising rates). It is entirely natural that platform owners will want to recoup some of the tremendous investment in building their platform – particularly the marketing costs – by charging high fees for the carriage of channels.

The most obvious charge is for the use of a platform's conditional access system. This gives access to the technology that checks whether a subscriber has paid their subscription, and allows the subscriber to view the channel if their credit is good. The BBC saw clearly, in the early days of platforms, that platform owners could exclude a particular brand or channel simply by adjusting this charge as they pleased.

Richard Brooke, who created his own platform within a platform, says that the EU has been visionary in its approach to access charges:

> Open access regulations in the UK and in Europe specifically relate to conditional access charging because the EU, under heavy lobbying by the BBC, focused on conditional access pricing and enshrined it in EU law. It's now enshrined in UK law that access pricing must be 'fair, reasonable and non-discriminatory'.

Brooke, who was working at BSkyB at the time, saw that this was a significant decision. It meant that not only could another operator establish a channel at reasonable cost on Sky – they could establish a whole series of channels, and manage their own subscribers, using Sky only as a delivery mechanism and for conditional access.

So DVC network was born:

> We were running this platform within a platform. It had various strands: it had a number of ethnic pay channels, it had adult pay channels. DVC network had radio stations, it had ethnic stations, it had free to air services and it had pay per view services, and its pay per view services were our own brand U>Direct. I have to say we recognised very clearly we were not going to be able to sustain the level of content acquisition and marketing in the long term. We were keeping it warm for a much bigger brand owner to come in and run it. We were in advanced negotiations for that to happen. Had we had an owner who was prepared to do that, it would have been a very big and profitable business.
>
> Turnover went from one million pounds in our first year of operation to eleven million in our second: it would have been twenty million in the third year, and that would have been more or less break-even. We were originally started up by Pearson Television. Pearson was sold to RTL and it was just that RTL did not want to know about digital television – they wanted to get hold of Channel 5 here in the UK.

The weakness of the proposition, as Brooke hints, is that the odd £378 million marketing spend per annum, in order to acquire and retain subscribers, makes it a big players' game. They needed a large company with enormous media ambitions to come in and take it over. Once RTL had decided that they were not going to pursue the model, the game was up. Once RTL had turned the proposition down it had little credibility.

Interestingly, the DVC Network channels were not branded as a complete package:

> DVC Network wasn't branded as a package on the Electronic Programme Guide because that was a good way for other brand owners to come in and take it over, since that was a very good way of putting your brand on the digital satellite. It was a reasonably sophisticated model.

However, the problem with this is that not building a brand often makes channel propositions less, and not more, attractive. If the audience can't even identify your channels, what gives the total package a value which is more than the sum of the parts? Brooke would argue that it made it easier for a brand to come in and place its own signature on the basket of channels – but that is not the way big media companies run their acquisition strategy. They want something which has a lot of tangible value – and which they can write down as such in their balance sheets. RTL was indeed after Channel 5, who had a huge and rising amount of brand goodwill and identity.

Platforms within platforms are hard to make work, and expensive to fund.

Who will win the digital world?

Peter Bazalgette is chairman of Endemol UK, one of the country's most successful independent producers. His company produces *Changing Rooms*, one of the mainstays of the BBC's weekday evenings, and *Big Brother*, based on a Dutch format, which creates audiences of 5 million viewers for Channel 4. I took him through the main current dilemmas for platform owners and independent producers alike. Peter offered some interesting insights – although bear in mind that he sees the industry, as he should, from the point of view of a large independent production house:

> The key issue at the moment is access. Channel owners are scared to death that platform owners are going to screw them. And BSkyB is

being investigated as to whether their pricing is fair. We've always said as independent producers that the spectrum owners have too much power. But the channel owners are now deploying against the platform owners the arguments that we use against the channel owners. The issue is access on fair terms.

Individuals are going to spend more on their media. The cake's going to be bigger, whatever people may think about there being no recognisable revenue model for an online business. True. But there's going to be a scramble for a share of this increasing cake. And it's absolutely impossible at the moment to predict who's going to get the most of that cake. They say content is king. But content is not king without access. Then they say Murdoch has the satellite platform – he's the power man. But it's not that simple. He's got to have the right bundle of channels. So what is the balance of power?

You've got a balance of power between platform owners, spectrum owners and intellectual property creators. Those are the three baronies. They have things in common and mutual antipathies. It's not possible at this stage to say how it's going to work out.

If you were setting up a digital television platform from scratch now, what content would you put on it?

The main things you would want on it are the terrestrial channels. You want the content that most people want. The old network channels.

But that doesn't make them subscribe to your platform. They can get them via a bent wire on the roof. If you are going to get people to switch from analogue to digital you've at least got to give them what they've already got.

Your best bet is to analyse why Murdoch's got the best proposition at the moment. Because he bought up movie rights and sports rights. He added 'must-see' things. You can order a pizza and look up your bank account, but no-one much cares about those things. You can do them in lots of other ways anyway. That's the simple answer. Murdoch took a big gamble but he got some must-see content.

And ITV Digital said 'It's about football and movies – so we also will do football and movies'. And they came third to market with the same content and failed.

> Yes, because the movies they bought were black and white movies and the football they bought was second division.

So what else is there? What else could they do?

> The business model of Endemol is not to be a broadcaster, and not to take the risks that Murdoch took. It is to look for collaborators and for access. We need the access, and once we've got it we're prepared to share in the revenue. Our business model as IP creators is not to be owners. That's as distinct from ITV, which is a vertically integrated model which purports to be a broadcaster, and was purporting to be a platform owner.
>
> Take the two cable companies in the UK – NTL and Telewest. Despite what they say about having to be content owners and creators as well as distributors, everything they say about having to own content will ultimately prove to be untrue. Their content arms will be sold off in twelve months and they will become telecoms companies. They will be carriers, that's all. They pass 50 per cent of the homes in Britain. Eventually someone – maybe it'll be Malone of Liberty Media – is going to get a fantastic asset and make a lot of money out of them. That applies to BT as well, which floated an idea about it making own content a few months ago (which it then withdrew). BT and the cable companies are going to be carriers, that's all. They're not going to buy content: they're going to facilitate the delivery of content.

What happens if, in the future, people have in their homes an electronic bucket into which they can draw lots of content? So the carriers become like the water companies, and companies like yours – Endemol – supply many different types of coloured water in the form of content. Then the world becomes yours, doesn't it?

> If I've got access to the bucket, number one. And if I've got the means to market my proposition, number two. So that people know it's there. Even when the old channels aren't channels anymore, which may happen, there will be a video library of destination entertainment, where I can go and find new releases. That will be gradual

because most people expect a schedule. But there will be a gradual transition to the networks becoming a library brand. And that's about marketing.

Some people think the future belongs to people who brand content. Like advertisers.

In reality, the future doesn't belong to anyone. But there are a number of players, and some are going to do better and some worse. If you assume the channel owners and the platform owners become the same, and that they both end up as carriers, you'll end up simply with carrying and with invention and production (the creation of intellectual property). Those are the two functions. Whose business model is going to take the best slice out of the television market? Maybe it hasn't been invented yet.

12. Interactivity

Interactivity is a feature new to television made possible by digital technology. It is the ability to send messages back to the broadcaster directly using the television technology as the carrier. Interactivity not using the television system as the carrier – for example by using a telephone – has been possible for some time. EMAP created a new business model using it, according to Richard Brooke, but the interactivity is largely illusory:

EMAP invented a new model in music television. They use premium rate telephony. The viewers, who are largely kids at home using their parents' phone, can ask for the next Kylie Minogue video using a premium rate number with absolutely no guarantee that it would come up in the play list – but at least it would make them feel it was interactive.

However, digital television technology allows viewers to signal choices back to the source of the broadcast using the programme controller in their hand. Although TPS in France have used this facility to allow viewers to talk to adverts – for example, booking a test drive for a car – interactivity is largely viewed with suspicion by existing broadcasters. Richard Brooke sums it up like this:

Interactive is one of those things which everyone got bored with as they couldn't get it to make money. But it works very well on the SkyDigital platform. Sky went through a process of setting up Sky television and of setting up an interactive service which was called 'Open . . .'. After a while they decided it was all one and the same thing and they put the two things together, and so 'Open . . .' is now part of Sky Television. The interactive services work well as part of an enhanced television service. So if you are watching Sky News you can go into Sky News active and look at the weather, or today in parliament or the sports news. But to have 'interactive' *per se* doesn't really excite people.

It seems that interactivity as a medium is so new and vulnerable that it can only be supported as part of something else. Interactivity has worked well in:

- *News:* Sky started the world's first interactive news service, where pieces from the night's news can be viewed at any time. This is true video on demand for news.
- *Factual programmes:* where background material can be supplemented by further information – as in the BBC's *Walking with Dinosaurs*.
- *Entertainment:* where quiz programmes can be simulated on an interactive channel where viewers can try a round themselves, as with ITV's *Who Wants To Be A Millionaire?*
- *Sport:* where interactivity can display a full set of results – and even give short highlights, such as winning goals.

All of these uses essentially enhance the brand, and the pull of the main channel from which they are derived. They do not, and cannot, stand alone. This makes them selling points for main channels and not viable as money-making ventures in their own right. In effect, one main digital news programme now has to have interactivity because a competitor has it. Interactivity at this stage of the development of digital television is added value – not a stand-alone medium.

However, it is not hard to imagine interactive content standing alone. For example, there are many business channels on digital television across the world – and very few of them are showing a profit. Business is essentially a subject for busy people, who don't have time to sit through twenty minutes of television to extract the information they need. Perhaps the best way to display business stories is to carry them as clips, which can be accessed on demand. This is technically possible – and is very popular in commercial applications, such as Reuters screens. Why has no one offered it to a domestic audience on digital television?

The answer may be that television entrepreneurs are mesmerised by the old channel model of television. They want to boast that they own a TV channel despite the fact that, like a yacht, it loses them money.

The fact is that interactive content as a medium is at the point of birth. We haven't seen it properly exploited yet. Eric Salama of WPP sees tremendous opportunities in a television model based on communities – and not on the broadcast model, which is very impersonal:

> I think the interesting growth areas are all to do with communities, and how the technology allows communities to form which have no basis geographically. I don't know if you've been ill or family members have been ill, but one of the main ways of finding out about illness now is talking to other people who have the same illness. I think that is a phenomenal breakthrough, which we haven't even begun to understand because it breaks down natural sources of authority. People are more likely to go onto a web site and find out who else has taken experimental drugs, as opposed to asking their doctor about it.
>
> I think the way that we can interact with individuals – and the way that we can get feedback from individuals, and research them – is very exciting.

So interactivity remains a model which represents an uncertain source of profit. But that is exactly what any commentator would have said about television in the United States in 1950. All it took was one individual to invent the quiz show and television, driven by advertising, started to make profits. That is what will happen with interactivity – all it requires is for someone to invent killer content for it.

Killer Operators

BOXED IN

Audiences now demand exactly what they want, when they want it – and also the feeling that the broadcaster is in touch with the beliefs and interests which characterise their community. Their television experience must be personal in order to impress them. So the successful digital television operator, the killer operator of the future, will have to use the technology to deliver the appearance of *personal content on demand.*

There is a dilemma in all current digital television technology: getting the technology to deliver personal content on demand at a reasonable price. Somewhere, somehow, you have to compromise in order to meet the demands of this new audience. At the time of writing, digital television operators are working feverishly on how to upgrade their systems. But, in the end, a system which is too pricey to sell or install will ruin an operator. So the race is on, not necessarily for the best technology but for commercially viable technology which also meets the high expectations of the digital television consumer.

There are currently two main methods of getting digital television into the home:

- On demand technology
- Direct to home technology.

Both technologies can exist on cable and satellite, although normally cable has a tendency to go for 'on demand' and satellite for direct to home (DTH). Digital terrestrial also tends to offer a version of DTH. There are a number of differences between the two modes.

On demand

On demand technology uses a very large server (a big computer with a large database) which sits within 25 miles of the homes it

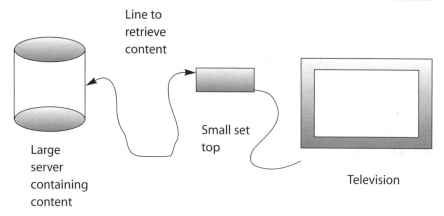

Figure 9.1. Model for on-demand programme delivery

serves. A large connection is established down the cable line (typically) between the server and the cable set top box.

The set top box in this system has a low specification and is essentially designed as a switch to the server, to pull bits of content down the cable line into the set top box and then show it on the television. The great advantage of this system is that it can be used to personalise the television experience with ease. Cable systems can have very elaborate user screens which will find a programme by your favourite director, or even by actors. It is also very simple to adapt to deliver *true* video on demand – where programmes are taken from a server as and when the viewer wants them. But video on demand delivered in this way is currently uneconomic for technical and business reasons.

Kingston Communications plc runs a state-of-the-art video on demand service delivered over broadband for the city of Hull in the north-east of England. They have ambitious plans to roll this out in other towns and cities. Dr Graham Wallace, their Director of Network Development, admits that video on demand is not commercially viable as a stand-alone service at present. There are two main reasons for this:

- The cost of the acquisition of content against the revenue from the number of people who actually use the service.
- The cost of setting up the hardware.

The cost of set-up includes building the mother and father of all servers – a machine capable of feeding 7,000 viewers simultaneously with video, down a 2-megabit/sec line to each of them. That's expensive, as Dr Wallace says:

> Our video on demand server, when we acquired it, was the largest in the world. That server cost a million pounds a couple of years ago, although costs are coming down by about 25 per cent a year. New video compression techniques like MPEG4 will also lower costs as they take up less bandwidth going into each house.

But video on demand, as the rights system works at the moment, only get 'first run' rights on movies six months after they have been released through video stores. Also, at the moment 70 per cent of revenues can go to the content owners. However, it does give a service that is irresistible to the new viewer:

> As a small standalone business, I find it quite hard to see video on demand working. But if you have large scale – and DSL is a technology of scale – it's fine. If you offer the triple play of telephony, high speed Internet and TV services (whether it's broadcast TV or video on demand or both) then the returns start to look very positive. I think video on demand is not the driver just at the moment, but I think it's something which can make an overall package quite exciting. At the very least, it can add a lot of stickiness to the service. You may not have a very big profit on video on demand – but you will make the service much more compelling.

Direct to home

Direct to home adapts one of the main principles of broadcasting, and applies it to the world of digital television. That principle is that sending many signals simultaneously to a lot of people makes economic sense, as it delivers economies of scale. Simultaneous broadcasting is harder to adapt to the demands of the new viewer – 'exactly what they want when they want it' – because it is much closer to the model of conventional broadcasting, where the play out centre determines what is sent to the viewer without consulting them. But, by tweaking the technology, it is possible to deliver *virtual* video on demand. Virtual video on demand delivered in this way is commercially viable, as direct to home's supporters are quick to point out. Making *virtual* video on demand as near as possible to *true* video on demand is the main drive behind developing direct to home systems at present.

Direct to home technology is an orgy of over-supply. The satellite method of delivery (the most common system) sprays all channels available simultaneously at a large footprint: one satellite can cover most of Europe. The fact that streams of all channels available to the subscriber are continuously hitting the satellite dish should make for a simpler set top box – but in fact the reverse is the case.

In 'direct to home' the set top box is smarter than its 'on demand' cousin, as the purpose of a direct to home box is twofold:

- To eliminate problems and issues of scale
- To move the user onto content as fast as possible.

In 'on demand' systems, like a cable system, the set top box works in conjunction with a local box in the street to select the channel

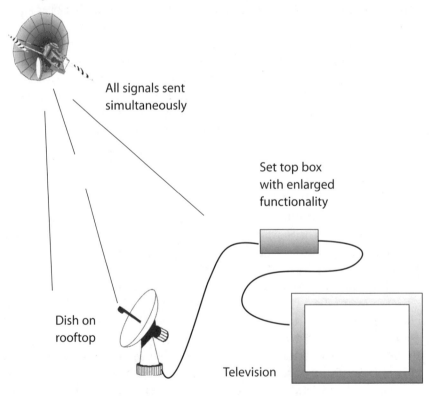

Figure 9.2. Model for direct to home programme delivery

coming into the home. Often the last hundred yards is a bottleneck which the technology gets around by sticking all the switching intelligence in the play out (i.e. the server and distribution) end of the system. In direct to home this is not the case as the play out end arrives, in all its multiplicity, in the satellite dish on the roof. What the set top box has to do, therefore, is to be as good a switching centre as all the play out machines in a cable system. This it does through the electronic programme guide, an elaborate and smart piece of software which allows the viewer to select, as fast as possible, the channel which they want decoded and sent to their set.

David Whittaker is a product development manager at NDS, the world's leading direct to home software suppliers. They are very proud of what they have achieved within the limitations of the set top box (the design of which is now five years old):

Sky has about 220 regular television channels, 50 radio channels and over 65 pay per view channels. The current Sky Electronic Programme Guide goes ahead 7 days. That means that 7,000 items are on the EPG at any one time. To provide both the listing information and the information synopsis would exceed the capacity of the box. However, we have overcome that problem.

The second issue is scalability. NDS saw early on that the disadvantage of on demand systems was the strain they put on getting the signal to as many households as possible:

The issue is 'how scaleable is that approach?' We already have a situation in the cable market where the idea that, when I press a button, a computer 25 miles away figures out what it is going to show me and displays it is becoming a challenge. NDS has always taken the view that we need to have maximum processing activity (so there's maximum efficiency) in the set top box. So on BSkyB I've got 5.9 million households receiving the Sky service – they can all go to the Electronic Programme Guide simultaneously. They can select a channel; they can move around completely autonomously because the system is completely scaleable. The actual extraction and display of the information which is relevant to the customer is taking place within the set top box.

In virtually all current deployed cable systems, as soon as you move into the information side of things – like electronic programme guides or interactivity – your button press will be sent back to a distant machine. That machine will decide what the button press will show you – and push that back to your individual box across shared resources which have to keep being expanded as you add viewers and users. In a direct to home system you have a situation where the button press is locally understood, and where the presentation of the information takes place locally on a private processor which is under your immediate control. That's because we have every element of what you might select coming down the satellite path. In the non-US market the people who provide the software in cable, who are called Liberate, have already recognised that the cable model is not sustainable. They are in the process of migrating their architecture to a system where data is delivered to the set top box, and the set top box extracts it.

If you're sharing a pipe with another thousand users, this involves assumptions about data capacity. You might draw comfort from the fact that you have a thousand users and they only draw a thousandth of the capacity of the pipe when they are looking at television. But, unfortunately, television viewing doesn't work like that. Everybody presses the electronic programme guide at 8 pm in the UK because a major soap opera has finished – and therefore dissipating load across a period of time doesn't work. Everyone always wants a fast responsive experience. You have big spikes. And big spikes at the points at which you least want them. Because from an advertising point of view you don't want viewers' eyeballs waiting for the electronic programme guide to wake up. You want a decision to transfer their channel attention and catch the advertising break on a channel. Because while NDS is seen as a pay TV system, in reality our technology is used just as much for the benefit of advertising-funded channels as it is for pay TV.

The direct to home architecture is therefore designed to allow the system to satisfy the new viewer, but without the operator incurring huge costs digging up the roads to install cables or buying the world's biggest video server. In effect, NDS provides the means for BSkyB (and DirecTV in the States) to provide programming within reasonable cost.

The challenges, however, come in moving direct to home technology out of 'broadcasting' (one size fits all) and into 'exactly what you want when you want it'.

GIVING THEM EXACTLY WHAT THEY WANT – AT A PRICE

Hardware is always an issue in making digital television pay. Consumers have grown accustomed from the PC market to having to upgrade their computers every two years as software becomes more and more extravagant in its use of memory and processing power. It does not take a genius to work out that this benefits manufacturers and software sellers more than it does consumers. However in the digital television market it would be suicide to upgrade hardware constantly – as requiring the consumer to purchase bigger and better set top boxes all the times will result in them not renewing their subscriptions. So a large part of the commercial success of digital television systems depends on how far software writers can extend the functionality of five-year-old boxes. Set top box software can be upgraded by downloads from the satellite or cable connection. For NDS the challenge is to extend the functionality of the present generation of set top boxes until they can go no further. And that means getting as far down the path to personalisation and virtual video on demand as they can within the limits of the box.

NDS identifies three features of the present generation of set top boxes that come close to video on demand:

- Near video on demand
- The electronic programme guide
- Subscriber versioning.

Near video on demand simply involves starting the most popular film available on pay per view every fifteen minutes. It normally takes up eight channels – as that is the capacity required to start a programme at that frequency. However, on satellite, it is entirely scaleable – in other words, any number of subscribers can watch the film simultaneously, as the channel carrying each start time is always present in the satellite feed.

Almost of greater importance to near video on demand is the speed with which a request to watch a pay per view movie is approved. This is achieved by having a credit account in the set top box:

> The NDS system runs a credit account effectively in the box, so when I say I want to watch that movie that processing takes place in the box – there's no need for the box to call home to check you're in credit. The box operates a credit capability. Once a month, the box will call home and report those items you purchased and then the credit account in the box is re-set.

The electronic programme guide not only allows swift migration to any channel you care to watch at the speed of light but it has also now been fitted with a personal planner. This allows the viewer to look ahead in the programme guide (which now runs to seven days) and bookmark a programme that they wish to watch. As the scheduled time of the programme approaches the guide warns the viewer that that programme is about to begin – and pressing on a button on the programme controller switches to it. The advantage of this system is that the electronic programme guide is constantly updated with programme changes, and so tracks your book-marked programme as it moves around the schedule.

Much subtler, and with profound implications for advertisers, is subscriber versioning. This exploits the fact that conditional access systems hold details of households subscribing to them. A simple way to divide subscribers up is by geography. It is possible, using the play out centre's knowledge of where subscribers live, to select different versions of main channels for them – so that in a certain slot reserved for a network on the EPG they see a particular version of that channel. David Whittaker describes how this works:

> The BBC uses the conditional access capability on Sky to select which of the four versions of BBC One is presented to you as a viewer. That means that you get the right personal, or local, news and weather service and it allows you to support certain business models. For example, if you are in Scotland you watch their premier league football because of the agreement the BBC has in Scotland. But elsewhere in the UK you are technically not aware that programme is even on air, and you are certainly not

allowed to watch it. Similarly, Channel 4 in the UK transmits six different versions of Channel 4 simultaneously. The programmes are always the same; the advertising breaks are different. The conditional access in the box selects and personalises which advertising grouping you're in so that you receive the correct version. Now that's done on a regional basis at the moment. Clearly the technology could be used to go to demographic groupings instead of regional.

The implications of this are that subscribers do not need to be segmented by geography – they can also be identified and targeted by income, type of household or even tastes in programming. So far, however, advertisers have only used this facility geographically.

There are also subtle forms of personalisation like parental access control, which allow parents to restrict access to certain channels through a four-digit personal identification number (PIN).

However, there is a limit to the new tricks which the present generation of set top boxes can be taught. They will simply run out of memory to accommodate new software. That is why a new generation of boxes is being introduced, available for a one-off payment and a monthly fee. When the manufacturing costs of these boxes come down, and when there is enough of an appetite for an upgrade within the existing subscriber base, these boxes will be sold at knock-down prices or possibly given away to subscribers. This will probably happen by the end of 2003.

The next generation of set top boxes has profound implications for how television will be viewed and, particularly, for television advertising.

TWO TUNERS AND A DISC

The next big leap forward, coming within the next twelve months, will be the mass rollout of new intelligent set top boxes. Boxes which don't merely offer the viewer a supermarket, but also build the supermarket to the specification of the individual shopper. This will be achieved by adding two tuners and a hard disc to the set top box. These additions, in one step, will bring the set top box much closer to a television 'digital hub' and a personal television supermarket.

The hard disc is there to record programmes, in data form, direct to a computer disc inside the set top box. The real breakthrough is that the set top box can be programmed to chase individual programmes around the electronic programme guide and record them as and when they are played out, regardless of whether you are watching them or even aware of them. The TiVo box (which features a hard disc) gives the viewer a much more comprehensive electronic programme guide than those of existing set top boxes: it not only gives fuller descriptions of programmes but also allows the viewer to rate programmes, so that the box can make a record of the viewer's tastes and preferences. The box then takes these tastes and preferences and hunts through the TiVo schedules for your favourites. Next time you tune in it says what it has recorded and invites you to view the shows. The only disadvantage is that the TiVo box only rings up its database once a day to update its programme guide, whereas electronic guides updated through the broadcast stream (like cable or satellite ones) are updated continuously. This can be important if a programme you are set to record moves its scheduled slot.

This is a brave experiment in personal choice. The business-minded management at NDS have decided not to go to those lengths of personalisation, simply because classifying programmes may be innately inaccurate and so lead to consumer disappointment. As David Whittaker points out:

> If you give viewers a list to classify their preferences – are all the attributes consistently described? How far down the cast list do you go? You ask it to show you a romantic comedy. But whose classification of a romantic comedy do you use? These are very great challenges.

There is also the facility for the TiVo box (and indeed for NDS's equivalent) to record programmes when instructed to do so by the subscriber management centre. This is fine when it is used to enhance the instant play out of a movie which is just fresh to pay per view, but is dubious when used to promote a failing television show. Strangely, the BBC pioneered this latter use in May 2002 when it forced the 50,000 TiVo boxes in the UK to record a situation comedy which was only attracting 1.5 million viewers. There was uproar. Granville Williams of the Campaign for Press and Broadcasting Freedom said:

This is an unwanted intrusion into people's lives. Consumers were told TiVo would give them greater control, yet the opposite has happened. Someone has decided 'This is what you want to watch'.[59]

While it is legitimate to use this facility to extend the ability of viewers to see popular programming (which helps viewers) it is clearly wrong to use it to promote minority shows. But this is a very grey area and raises important questions about recording initiated by the subscription centre.

The importance of adding two tuners to the box cannot be understated. It is in the architecture of the new NDS box, called XTV. XTV is a business-to-business product and is then sold by platforms owners under their own branding. In the UK, BSkyB sell it as Sky Plus. David Whittaker describes the thinking behind the architecture:

The most obvious next place the box can go is adding storage and a second tuner. That's designed to improve the choice to the viewer. It allows the viewer to record one programme while watching another. It also allows them to pause a live television programme. It means your children can go and eat a meal when it's ready – rather than when the TV schedule will allow you to have the meal.

Both tuners can go to the disc. One is making a recording of some other programme. The other is making a recording of the programme you are notionally watching live. But you've chosen to come back to it late. So then you can un-click the pause button and the tuner will take to you to a recording of the programme you started watching live.

The notion is a simple one – two tuners offer you all the following options:

- To record something else while you are watching a programme (the fact that you couldn't do this with the first generation of set top boxes was a major consumer criticism).
- To be able to ask the box to record all programmes of a certain type while you carry on watching the set top box regardless of what it is seeking and recording.

- To be able to pause a live programme and then return to it if you are interrupted. This works by recording the programme you started to watch when you hit the pause button. When you return to the 'paused' live programme and play it, you are in fact watching a recording.
- The set top box is capable of using the second tuner to record material which it sends down from the satellite while you are using the other tuner to watch television.

This last use is the one with which the BBC has probably scored a world first by finding a way of abusing it! However, it was created specifically by NDS to open up new business opportunities:

> One of the reasons we specified two tuners on our new XTV box is that when the tuner isn't being used by the viewer there may be business opportunities. We can use it to deliver extra content to the disc in a secure manner. We can have a situation where whenever the new hot movie comes out, whereas a video on demand service would require a large server and lots of connectivity to the set top box, we can store the movie automatically on the disc. So they can view that hot movie, on demand, under pay TV. When the next Julia Roberts movie comes out, because Julia Roberts movies are always hot movies, there's an opportunity to send that movie to the set top box the night before. So when that movie is released, at say seven o'clock, the demand to see it can be completely without constraint. All your viewers can go to it and watch it. However, if you go to a true video on demand service not everyone can watch the movie at seven on a Friday night because you haven't go the capacity to deliver it.

This is what is meant by 'virtual' video on demand. The Julia Roberts movie in this example appears to be playing down at the demand of the viewer – but in reality it is coming off their box from the time at which it becomes available, and not from a distant play out centre. As far as the viewer is concerned there is no difference, even though technically the system he or she is using is not a 'true' video on demand system.

NDS is able to release 'remote recorded' movies at specified times because, unlike the TiVo box, they can enlist the use of the conditional access software in the XTV box. The XTV box, unlike the TiVo, records downloaded programmes fully encrypted – and the viewers only pay for them if they choose to watch them. This is possible as the conditional access software is already in the XTV box. Therefore, it would be possible to record a whole series of encrypted movies – which the viewer's programme guide would show were available to be played on demand, but which the viewer may not choose to watch. In that case they would not be charged for the download. The download facility merely exists to create video on demand:

> Because we are so strong on the conditional access side of things, we record the content in its original scrambled form. Then we only apply the business access rules at the point at which it is viewed. This may seem very mundane, but what it means is that premium content such as pay per view movies can be recorded at no financial commitment cost to the viewer. I can now record all the pay per view movies which might be interesting to me during the week so on a Friday night I can have a choice of five or six of them – and I don't have to wait quarter of an hour for them. They will play immediately, and have pause capability.

This will make the XTV box, and its relatives, real pieces of killer hardware. They will out-manoeuvre true video on demand systems (with large servers back at the play out area) simply because they will be able to offer video on demand to the viewer, at a cost to the operator which is a fraction of delivering *true* video on demand. That is why it is inevitable that when News Corp (who owns eighty per cent of NDS) wishes to assert their lead over cable and DSL systems it will simply drop the prices of the new boxes and roll them out. This will give them unassailable added value and reinforce their market leadership in digital television technology.

At the moment video on demand is not being promoted very heavily simply because 'on demand' operators know a large take-up will add to their running costs:

> At the moment there's relatively little marketing going on for video on demand presentation because, despite the hype, the roll-out of video on demand is relatively small. I still can't find anyone reporting profitable activity in video on demand and pushing its deployment. Most video on demand deployments, particularly in the States, have tended to be synonymous with

getting fresher content – which is a significant business challenge to overcome as you have to convince the movie people to provide you with that fresh content. And there's a limit to the amount of fresh content there is anyway.

But the day is soon coming when *virtual* video on demand will rule the digital airwaves.

THE DEATH OF THE CHANNEL

TiVo and XTV boxes are known generically as Personal Video Recorders or PVRs (although there is a lot more to them than that – as this chapter has shown). PVRs have a serious and hidden consequence for channel owners – surveys of their use show that 70 per cent of people abandon live viewing as soon as they start to use them. That destroys the main driver of channel revenue – the advertising break. Those same surveys also show that viewers who abandon 'live' viewing also speed through advertising breaks. In fact, there is much evidence that one of the first ways in which PVRs modify behaviour is that viewers deliberately start to watch live programmes ten minutes late. This gives the box enough time to allow the viewer to zap through all the advertising breaks.

This is incredibly bad news for television networks, which rely on the advertising generated by their channels for the majority of their revenue. It is also dire news for advertising agencies who are very reliant on large spends on television advertising.

Rahul Chakkara created some of Proctor and Gamble's first interactive adverts for the French digital channel TPS. He is now Director of Interactive TV for NDS. To the question '*How do you get viewers to watch advertising content when they're not compelled to?*', he has an arresting answer:

I don't know.

I wish I had the answer, and I think that everyone who is out there in the market saying that they have the answer is bullshitting. No one knows. The only way we can know the answer is by actually doing things and finding out. Right now we are approaching some of the advertisers here to find the answer – there is a lot of speculative talk and no-one knows. I believe the answer will be different from any of the speculation current at the moment.

Clients [product owners] see the need for this and know this is going to impact their business. They also know it's not going to impact their business for the next twelve months. They're not doing much at the moment as the penetration [of PVRs] is not that high. But everyone clearly realises it's going to impact. There is a lot going on which is not exposed to the public. The people who crack this and find the answers first will have a huge competitive advantage.

In summary: at the point at which PVRs are rolled out in any volume, channels which are heavily reliant on advertising breaks for their revenue are going to have great difficulty. Their business model is dead. They have about twelve months to think up a new one.

The End of the Beginning

The first forty years of television were an aberration. It was a strange world, constrained by an absence of any fundamental technological change. Its best side was that it delivered moving pictures into the home. Its dark side was that it tried to suggest to viewers that it was good for them to receive 'channelised' television, where cultural tsars dictated the order in which programmes could be viewed – and, indeed, what the overall universe of programmes should be on any one day.

But it was simply a long beginning. That beginning is now over.

The persistence of arguments for the retention of the old regime are now simply amusing. They are still prevalent in Europe, where it is argued that people like to have to sit and watch a programme all at the same time because 'then they can talk about it in the bar the following day'. This quaint notion of a mass labour force disappearing collectively into a bar to discuss something which they were all sitting at home watching simultaneously the previous evening betrays a contempt for viewers. It belongs in a sentimental view of human behaviour which was probably last true in the 1920s, at the height of the age of mass production. It is a world which is unrecognisable today.

There is also a strange argument that, by resisting the advance of digital television technology, we will somehow preserve our individual cultures. This argument is strongest in France, where it goes under the name of the 'cultural exception'. It has caused French media giant Vivendi huge problems, as Vivendi realised that digital television in particular simply let people watch exactly what they wanted to watch – much to the detriment of dull subsidised French films. At the heart of this argument is the fear that digital technology advances the spread of American-made programming. It does – but only because people seem to find it superior, in many cases, to their domestic fare. It is not a powerful argument to say to people at the beginning of the twenty-first century that because it is interesting you cannot watch it. The technology is now here to allow them to ignore you.

In truth, conventional channel television limited to four or five channels was doomed from the point at which viewers encountered their first supermarket. Just because people watch television does not mean that they do not exist as consumers (as many broadcasting executives seem to forget). The supermarket introduced the consumer to the notion that they could get exactly what they wanted when they wanted it. Fresh from the producer. What was odd about television technology was how long it took to catch up with the new consumerism.

With digital, television technology has leapt past the supermarket model into a world in which consumers not only have infinite choice – but also one in which technology can deliver a supermarket personal to them. Digital television technology is like walking down the road and discovering that every time you go through the door of your supermarket the shelves have been re-arranged, so that products you like are in easy reach. The simple example of sending you the relevant version of a national channel so that its advertising is aimed at your demographic is a modest example of this. The capabilities of the next generation of set top boxes are an outstanding example.

This book has tried to emphasise that it is not the technology which has produced the new viewer. Viewers changed first – and then found developments like digital television so useful to their lifestyles that they took them up rapidly. Until quite recently, broadcasters in the US believed that people were prepared to pay nothing for new television technology. But today they are prepared to up to $100 a month simply for more television and more technological features. This speaks of the emergence of a viewer who was, at the very least, severely misunderstood for some time.

The other important headline in this book is that now new digital television technology is established the next generation are using it in ways no-one imagined – and with a ferocity with which even the set top box developers can hardly keep pace. The new, perhaps the greatest, age of television is only just beginning.

Television is now adopting its most plastic form. It can truly be all things to all people as it is rapidly acquiring the capability to seem to be about you, the viewer. This has some immediate implications: for politics, for viewers, for investors, for advertisers and for broadcasters.

Interview with Greg Dyke

Greg Dyke was appointed Director General of the BBC in 2000. Previously he was the CEO of Pearson Television, a major independent production company. Before that he was Director of Programmes of London Weekend Television.

He has transformed the BBC from a moribund public service broadcaster into a dynamic ratings winner. It was hard to understand why it had never previously overtaken its main television rival, ITV, in the ratings because the BBC enjoys an income from a television tax (the licence fee) that generates £2.5 billion a year. However this year, for the first time, it did indeed overtake a troubled and cash-strapped ITV in the ratings.

Greg has also announced plans for a whole series of properly funded digital television channels (that is channels which are only available through digital receivers). These include a rival to Channel 4, BBC4, and proposals for a youth channel to rival Viacom's Nickelodeon.

In partnership with BSkyB plc he has led the BBC to success in the auction of the digital terrestrial franchises. These became available when ITV Digital went into administration earlier this year with losses on digital terrestrial of £1.2 billion.

He spoke to the author in an interview on 8 July 2002.

Alan: Who do think will be the ultimate winners in digital television? Do you think it will be content makers, channels or platform owners?

Greg: It could be no one. Rupert Murdoch said at one stage that he hadn't yet seen a model where any business made any more money out of digital TV. He might be right. Clearly people selling boxes ought to make more money.

Alan: Pace isn't.

Greg: Bad answer! It could be nobody. Of course the BBC isn't in it for money. By winners you mean making a profit?

Alan: Yeah.

Greg: The consumer is probably the only winner. Because the consumer will have more choice. If that's winning, it will be the consumer. I'm not convinced that Sky will ever make the level of return on capital that it was before. I've talked to people like Sony and they believe that as they're investing a lot they're going to get a return. It could be nobody though in terms of money – but the consumer gets considerably more choice.

Alan: Weren't broadcasters better off before their technology got mixed up with computer technology?

Greg: Yes, if you were a traditional terrestrial broadcaster funded by advertising or by a licence fee you were better off without masses of extra channels. But that wasn't realistic. But certainly in the responses of recent weeks from ITV, you realise that the reason they were in digital transmission was they were desperately trying to close down a market – so that no one came into digital terrestrial to compete with them. Which is why they lost. Yeah it was completely defensive. And you understand why. I think if I was in their position I might have done the same thing.

Alan: An expensive way of doing it.

Greg: But they went the other way – in trying to compete with pay TV. They then got into this semi-schizophrenic position where they couldn't work out what their job was. Was their job to defend their terrestrial channels, or was it to increase the number of pay homes? And you saw it with Channel 4 last week. The reason Channel 4 didn't join our consortium was they were desperate to get pay homes available for their pay TV channels. But actually if you look at what happens to Channel 4's audience in digital pay homes, it wasn't in their interest to get more pay homes. So there's a conflict always for terrestrial commercial channels.

Alan: Why did digital terrestrial television fail in the UK?

Greg: It failed for a number of reasons. The technology was crap. It didn't work. When we did the work on it we discovered that only 39 per cent of people in the UK could receive it, and half of those got interference. Two, from the moment the European Commission threw Sky out of the original digital terrestrial consortium for being anti-competitive, that was probably the moment that Carlton and Granada should have given the licences back. They then took a decision to go head-to-head with Sky – which was lunacy. And finally there is no model in the world that we can find where three competing pay platforms all make money.

Alan: Why will the BBC digital terrestrial proposition wash its face (i.e. break even)?

Greg: It's much, much cheaper. It won't wash its face   but it won't lose much money. We are going to put the digital converter in the television sets. So you go to the shop – you buy the television set you plug it in. If it doesn't work you go back to the manufacturer or the shop – you certainly don't come to the broadcaster. So you don't have to have that whole infrastructure of support, any of that stuff at all – it's just an appliance.

Alan: What you're saying is it's going to have an element of subsidy because it will never make the revenues from the sale of the boxes or from the advertising to cover the cost of the operation?

Greg: No we're not even involved in the sale of the boxes, nothing to do with us. They're like television sets. The BBC was about to spend an extra sum of money anyway taking additional digital television capacity on Channel 5, so we could do interactive. Our model won't make sense because whatever we do costs money 'cos we don't raise any. Sky will lose money in the early years but will obviously hope that if enough of these take off they will make money in the later years. Crown Castle are interested in channels paying for their broadcasting – their masts and towers. So the total cost, by the standards of what's been lost before, is very, very small.

Alan: The argument would also go that this is better way of increasing reach for your new digital channels?

Greg: Well we have a real problem if the government doesn't believe in analogue switch off. How do we justify a lot of channels which people can't get? Now I happen to believe that what's happening on DTT now makes analogue switch off more likely not less likely. Because the £50 box will come down to a £20 adapter and with that you can deal with all the other sets in the home as well

Alan: What do you think is the real driver which makes people take up digital television?

Greg: I don't think there's any driver. I think they're completely confused. I think the driver is solely more choice. But they don't know whether it's digital or not digital. They want more stuff. The word digital doesn't mean anything to anybody. When we market our digital terrestrial TV service, if we market anything which mentions digital we should be shot.

Alan: How will you market it?

Greg: More ordinary tele. Not those words but that concept. More ordinary tele for free.

Alan: Isn't there a danger in saying something's free – as if it's free it implies it has no value?

Greg: People are used to free television.

Alan: · Free at the point of delivery.

Greg: People are used to it. They understand exactly what you mean. The research we did showed us that the hardest sell will be the people who don't want pay television and don't believe it's free. They think it's a catch. They think you get the box – and somehow someone a year later is going to come round and start charging you. Which is why we wanted to have a proposition which had no pay television on it.

Alan: I am not sure that anyone can rely on a share of subscription and advertising anymore to make a channel work in digital television. Has that model gone away in terms of digital?

Greg: In all the channels we tried to give up being part of pay television and to come onto free digital television, none of them would come. So the UK Golds, the Sky Ones and the rest of it. The subscription income for the next five years was much too important for them. So there is no doubt that advertising is a supplement for pay but it's not a replacement for pay.

Alan: How important will channels be in the future. Will people still go for a schedule?

Greg: Yes. Because it's what the viewer knows. I've seen too many years of engineers coming up with wonderful plans. It will take a long time to change people's viewing habits. There's still a large demand for someone else to schedule it for you. TiVo is certainly doing personal scheduling. The people I know who have TiVo says it changes your life. I've got a TiVo – I've never quite plugged it in. If you can make it all simpler then personal TV is a possibility. All the work that was done here predicting what was ten years ahead isn't what's happening.

Alan: The thing that fascinates me about TiVo is that if 70 per cent of people using them don't follow the schedule, and skip through the ad breaks, what happens to spot advertising?

Greg: The commercial channels driven by advertising are clearly going to have a terrible time anyway. First because there is a massive downturn in advertising – but that could be cyclical, although I doubt it. Secondly, if you lose share year in year out, which they are doing, you fall off the cliff.

Alan: What would you do if you were Head of Granada right now?

Greg: I think I would top myself. The whole of ITV has to be re-thought. ITV is in free fall at the moment. It's lost four share points this year. I don't see any evidence of anybody in ITV who is going to change that. There are people there who could – but they're not running it. But all this stuff's cyclical. Their time will come again. They've got to re-think the business model.

Alan: It's not clear what that should be?

Greg: I think you've got to assume you are no longer such a large mass audience channel. You've got to assume that the downturn in advertising is not cyclical but is actually real. You've got a new cost base and you've got to work it out from there. That's our new cost base – it grows by 2 per cent a year real. That's our cost base – how do we run this service?

Alan: What does it mean for public service broadcasting?

Greg: On commercial channels it means there'll be less of it. That's inevitable. That's what happens in fragmenting marketplaces. Regulators and politicians all hate that. They think they can have the best of all worlds and they can't. In some of the discussions we had about pay on DTT the politicians said to us, 'we want a third pay platform'. I said, 'You wanted a car industry – but you haven't got one.' That's life. Politicians only want to embrace the market when it suits them. Here they've got the market and they didn't like the results.

Alan: Broadband – DSL – is getting into quite a few early adopted houses. Not bad if you have a bucket in the attic which takes video and audio content for getting it there. Is that realistic in the long term?

Greg: Yeah. What we are doing in Hull is quite interesting. What broadband will be able to do in communities is quite interesting. And the market won't fund that. There is no doubt that what you can do in terms of education, in terms of communities with broadband, is fascinating. It's much further away than anybody thought. When I got here at the height of the dot com boom we spent all our time thinking 'we're the most visited site in Europe – how can we turn it into a commercial business?' Two years on, the supply of content onto the web has no business model. There are business models on the web – but they are not supplying information.

Alan: Given that, it puts the BBC model in rather a good position – because you can afford to supply free information over the Internet. Could you sell the BBC model in America?

Greg: It's a funny place America. I sat next to an American woman recently who said, 'I think the BBC is communistic'. I said, 'I never think you're going to understand'. I think they are so hostile to taxation to public good it's quite difficult. But I do think in the next charter for renewal of the BBC we need to discuss what is the opportunity for a publicly funded content provider nationally and locally. Locally is particularly interesting I think.

POLITICS

The change in society is being hastened by changes in communications technology, like the introduction of digital television. Television has always been an important medium for politicians, and they will find the changes in television technology tough:

1. It will be hard for political parties to preach to viewers using television. If they assume they are talking to a great mass of like-minded people they will be ignored. That is not how the new television viewer either thinks or acts. Nor does the technology compel them to do anything other than acquire a set of opinions which, like a set of clothes, they find useful for a season and then discard.
2. There will be issues and causes which television allows people to adopt and follow. But they will not be allied to any political set of beliefs. The technology will simply let you track them and, when they cease to appeal, the viewer can move onto something else.
3. This fragmentation of strongly held ideas and beliefs will be aided by the new television technology. There may come a time when the sheer choice and personalisation of television will spur an increase in fragmentation and choice in politics. There will be many more, smaller parties, as only in that way can politics reflect the spread of views and their tendency to change with rapidity. They will be dealing with a population with 'strong beliefs, lightly held' – abetted by a television culture which encourages this stance.

VIEWERS

The viewer is set to become even more unreasonable and demanding. The veil will fall from their eyes. They will realise that they no longer have to accept any compromise in television content – and that if they are stuck for ideas of what to watch, their television equipment will supply them with something which appeals to their tastes. That is the way in which TiVo technology is moving, and also NDS's new generation of boxes (XTV).

The idea of the television as an intelligent servant, rather than a benign dictator in the corner of one room, will take time to sink in.

But when it does, it is likely that a super-intelligent television will offer up games, pictures and family movies, in addition to television fare, and send them to other devices around the house. *Working* to find something to watch or do electronically will fade away.

Where the viewer will exercise judgement is in the choice of his or her content provider. In fact, if any conversation does take place in bars it will be far more concerned not with what was watched last night, but with the satellite or cable package to which people subscribe. And people are not merely discussing which channels they can receive: they are also concerned with packaged services such as broadband Internet access. The hunt for the ideal electronic content company has started. It may well end up with the equivalent of an electronic cistern in the house, into which all relevant content is pumped through as many electronic pipes as the viewer finds relevant to their lifestyle.

INVESTORS

Investors have been badly blind-sided by the rapid change in television technology. They are unsure of where it will go next. Investors tended, rather lazily, to see growth and value in the old television networks. But with viewers' relationship to advertising undergoing such a rapid change, and with the rapid decline in the audience share of the networks, the networks offer very dubious value.

There are now only three correct bets in media investment:

- In content providers who can appeal to the distinct communities which can be reached using the digital media.
- In platform owners who understand how to develop technology which is commercially viable, and to acquire attractive content at the right price.
- In content brand builders who understand how to operate in the digital environment, developing content or channels which achieve cult status or become hits in their own right.

In the first category, as stated in the previous chapter, Viacom is emerging as a clear-sighted and visionary winner. In the second category News Corp, and its BSkyB, Star and NDS subsidiaries, are the corporations that have got the difficult blend of technology and content consistently right. Platform owning is such a difficult business in which to be successful that it is one of the great wonders of the twenty-first century that News Corp has done so well. It must have been due to judgement and not luck, however. Digital platforms are too complicated to leave to luck.

The third category is the hardest to define. Digital television clearly demands skills in building branded content. It is hard to believe that this will be the exclusive preserve of independent producers, rights owners or platform owners. It used to be the preserve of the channel owners – who would commission a show, place it in the schedule and promote it. However, digital television offers viewers the ability to select what they see, and to learn about it from other digital media. It may be an area into which advertisers – or multimedia owners like AOL Time Warner or CNN (or indeed the BBC) – eventually move. In a market in which platform owning is very hard to get right, and being an independent producer is subject to terrible risks, brand building will probably be the most profitable area in which to operate.

As with so much in the digital television industry, however, the old is still dying and the new has yet to be born. But to anyone who wishes to make money, branding – multimedia 'content amplification' – is a vacuum still to be properly filled even by the big media companies.

Finally, a word of warning to those who are tempted by technology which appears to offer platform owners (like cable or satellite) a new set top box, or a new system for providing personalisation to viewers. Don't invest. The only successful way to win at technology is to be a successful platform owner. Platform owners take critical decisions about technological features and developments *which fit into the business plan of the platform*. A stand-alone software business cannot conform exactly to someone else's business plan unless they are owned by them (as NDS is by News Corp). Microsoft's attempts to penetrate the television software market have foundered on this problem (which is why they are now trying to penetrate the 'entertainment hub' industry using Xbox). So when someone shows you some software to personalise television – decline the opportunity.

ADVERTISERS

Advertisers, unless they are very smart indeed, are going to get the worst of the digital television revolution. The risk is simple. Sixty per cent of current campaign budgets are spent on television advertising. Advertising agencies take a percentage of that (it can be as much as 15 per cent of advertising spend). But the networks are failing to deliver the mass audiences of which they were once capable so advertising rates have fallen – and with it the amount the agency takes. Worse, the television audience is fragmenting and personalising so rapidly that it is highly unlikely that advertisers will see the same scale of spends again, as clients spend less on a multiplicity of low cost channels.

But there is even worse news. The new set top boxes (as the last chapter showed) now mean that 70 per cent of viewers ignore (i.e. speed through) adverts completely.

So what is to be done? The answer is that the killer application for digital television advertising has yet to be devised. The problem is that most solutions proposed so far involve taking the viewer away from television content to some kind of 'advertising zone'. This annoys the programme owners. Intelligent solutions involve 'paying' the viewer for their attention by reducing the cost of a pay per view movie or event if viewers watch the advertisements. There is the intriguing possibility of using the subscriber base to isolate viewers demographically (all households earning over $50,000, for example) but this assumes that people will still continue to watch channels. The evidence suggests that they won't.

Advertisers are going to have to decide what business they are in. If it is 'publicity' then they will have to consider new ways of reaching audiences, either through sponsoring television content or through making it themselves. If they are in 'branding' (i.e. giving products an identity) they would be better entering the arena of tying up complex deals where content appears across several digital media, and so builds a brand. They should take a percentage of the sales rights of the branded content. Only then they will not be in advertising. Perhaps, given the prognosis, that is just as well.

BROADCASTERS

Broadcasters will continue to have a very uncomfortable time, unless they are among the clear winners who are emerging – companies who have their digital strategies correct to the extent that they are now assuming positions of market leadership.

The most threatened species are the traditional networks: the CBSs, the ITVs, the ABCs, the RTFs. Some of these (like ABC, who are owned by Disney) are owned by bigger corporations who will weather the storm as they are so strong in other fields. But the networks are businesses which must now decide which slot they are going to occupy in the digital television market. Saying that they are 'networks' is not a good enough strategy.

The networks' problem is that they are losing audience share at a rate that in any other business would mean sale or closure. They are also classically 'stuck in the middle' between the increasing power of the successful platform owners and the demands of rights owners with successful hits or talent. The only space they occupy naturally is that of 'brand content management' – as traditionally they have been good at commissioning content, positioning it and promoting it so that its value is boosted. However, their success in this field has been counteracted by two common mistakes:

- Their reluctance to pay for world rights when commissioning a programme
- Their failure (particularly in Europe) to try to sell their product to global markets.

The excuse that it is hard to create product for global markets from small scale – almost cult – programming has been disproved by the success of Grundy Television in Australia and Viacom's MTV. However, both Grundy and MTV got very good at taking a core of material and then localising it for different markets. Grundy even used to take soap formats (like *Neighbours*) and created different versions for different territories. There is much to be learnt by the networks about the creation of a strong electronic brand, and then re-versioning it for distribution from a central store. This, with the advent of electronic hubs in the home, is what content providers will have to excel at – so that the hub can send your brand to a personal planner with the same facility that a television version arrives on a television monitor.

The only companies who have fully embraced this concept are games manufacturers, with properties like Lara Croft and Poké-mon springing up across many media.

The future – particularly the 'hub in the home under the stairs' (as described by Dr Graham Wallace) – will see significant reduction in people's desire to watch television arranged as channels. We know this from surveys of how people with a hard disc in their set top box view television. *Seventy per cent do not watch channels.* They watch programmes. It is very hard for the networks to get their minds around this idea, as it flies in the face of 40 years of experience. But experience, in this case, will let the networks down. They have to think outside the channel mindset and come up with a new role and vision. Channel 4's strategy of starting even more channels is similarly flawed. The networks must, at the very least, think of themselves as programme brand builders or they are doomed.

This book has been very sceptical that digital *terrestrial* television can work as a pay TV business. The technology, as it has been designed so far, is not sufficiently robust. However, it is entirely possible that it would work as a means of carriage for free to air channels. In all countries, there is a sufficient range of channels which are free at the point of delivery to create the thirty or so channels which a subscription-free digital terrestrial service would require to make it viable. Revenue would then be generated by sales of set top boxes and the carriage fees paid to the operator by the content owners.

Of all the broadcasters operating in digital television at present, only two clear winners are emerging:

- News Corp, through its NDS, BSkyB and Star subsidiaries
- Viacom, through MTV and other content brands like Nickelodeon.

Viacom has a clear vision of itself as a content provider (*not* as a channel provider). Its strategy of building a very expensive content re-purposing system with IBM demonstrates this. It has also learnt an important management trick – giving local television territories enough headroom to listen to their audiences and produce enough local content to make the audience watch. Many US operations in particular are very bad at releasing enough head-office control to allow local Vice Presidents to connect with their audiences in this way. But in Viacom's case it has reaped dividends.

A special mention has to go to EMAP for doing some innovative experiments with different revenue models for digital television. It is not clear if the long-term model for their channel The Box – where viewers select records through premium line phone calls – is sustainable, but it is certainly an interesting idea which is not costing them anything. There will need to be many more interesting ideas over the next decade from cheeky entrants like EMAP (whose core business is magazine publishing).

However, the outright winner in digital television platforms is shaping up to be Rupert Murdoch's News Corp. This really is a remarkable achievement, as it has involved getting five things absolutely correct from a standing start in a field in which there was little or no previous experience (and certainly no business books!):

- The rights deals (like the football and the movies)
- The marketing (persuading a sceptical media that viewers wanted exactly what they want when they want it)
- The channel deals and variety
- The customer care and subscription management
- The technology (which, as this book has been at pains to point out, is far from easy to get right first time).

Given that News Corp, through acquiring NDS and successfully building brands like BSkyB and Star, has hit all these goals they clearly have a business model which works. And that is an unusual thing in any industry which is just five years old. It is hard to conclude that they are anything other than unstoppable.

How News Corp managed this is probably a big enough subject for another book. However, Murdoch has always been willing to admit mistakes early and act on them. At the time of writing he looks as though he will finally acquire the Telepiu pay network in Italy, although his investment in Germany did not come off. He will probably be back snapping at the heels of DirecTV in the US if Echostar can't acquire it.

He is also ruthless with management who seem to have lost focus. They get paid off early (and generously). It is an old-fashioned management model, but it works.

But the overall winner in digital television is the viewer. They will finally gain in television the same freedom and power as they would get as if they had a supermarket built every day dedicated to their tastes and desires. It is a change that will have profound implications – not only for television, but also for the way in which the world communicates. Real television has only just started.

Channels available in the $81.99 package offered by DirecTV, May 2002

A&E
ABC Family
Action
All News Channel
American Movie Classics
Animal Planet
BBC America
The Biography Channel
Black Entertainment Television
BLACK STARZ!
Bloomberg Television
Boomerang
Bravo
Cartoon Network
The Church Channel
Cinemax
Cinemax West
CNBC
CNN
CNN/Sports Illustrated
CNNfn/CNN International
Comcast SportsNet (Mid-Atlantic)
Comedy Central
Country Music Television
Court TV
C-SPAN
C-SPAN 2
Daystar
Discovery Channel
Discovery Civilization

Discovery Health Channel
Discovery Home & Leisure
Discovery Kids Channel
Discovery Wings
Disney Channel East
Disney Channel West
Do It Yourself Network
Empire Sports Network
E! Entertainment Television
Encore East
Encore West
ESPN
ESPN CLASSIC
ESPN 2
ESPNEWS
FLIX
Food Network
Fox Movie Channel
Fox News Channel
Fox Sports Net Arizona
Fox Sports Net Bay Area
Fox Sports Net Chicago
Fox Sports Net Cincinnati
Fox Sports Net Detroit
Fox Sports Net Florida
Fox Sports Net Midwest
Fox Sports Net New England
Fox Sports Net New York
Fox Sports Net North
Fox Sports Net Northwest
Fox Sports Net Ohio
Fox Sports Net Pittsburgh
Fox Sports Net Rocky Mountain
Fox Sports Net South
Fox Sports Net Southwest
Fox Sports Net West
Fox Sports Net West 2
Fox Sports World
FX
Galavision
Game Show Network

The Golf Channel
Hallmark Channel
HBO
HBO Family
HBO Family West
HBO2
HBO2 West
HBO Signature
HBO West
Headline News
The Health Network
The History Channel
History International
Home & Garden Television
Home Shopping Network
The Independent Film Channel
The Learning Channel
Lifetime
Lifetime Movie Network
Love Stories
Madison Square Garden (MSG)
MoreMAX
The Movie Channel East
The Movie Channel West
MSNBC
MTV
MTV2
MuchMusic
Music Choice: 70s
Music Choice: 80s
Music Choice: Alternative Rock
Music Choice: American Originals
Music Choice: Atmospheres
Music Choice: Big Band
Music Choice: Body & Soul
Music Choice: Blues
Music Choice: Channel X
Music Choice: Classic Country
Music Choice: Classic Light
Music Choice: Classic R&B
Music Choice: Classic Rock

Music Choice: Classical Masterpieces
Music Choice: Contemporary Christian
Music Choice: Dance
Music Choice: Easy Listening
Music Choice: For Kids Only
Music Choice: Gospel
Music Choice: Hit List
Music Choice: Jazz
Music Choice: Light Jazz
Music Choice: Metal
Music Choice: New Releases
Music Choice: Progressive
Music Choice: R&B Hits
Music Choice: Rap
Music Choice: Rock Hits
Music Choice: Showcase
Music Choice: Showcase II
Music Choice: Singers & Standards
Music Choice: Soft Rock
Music Choice: Solid Gold Oldies
Music Choice: Sounds of the Season
Music Choice: Today's Country
Music Choice: World Beat
Mystery
National Geographic Channel
The National Network
NBA TV
New England Sports Network
Newsworld International
Nickelodeon/Nick at Nite (East)
Nickelodeon/Nick at Nite (West)
Noggin/The N
Outdoor Life Network
Oxygen
PAX
PBS KIDS Channel
PBS YOU
QVC
Regional Sports Network
SCI FI Channel
The Science Channel

Shop At Home
ShopNBC
SHOWTIME East
SHOWTIME Extreme
SHOWTIME Showcase
SHOWTIME TOO
SHOWTIME West
SoapNet
Speed Channel
STARZ!
STARZ! Theater
STARZ! West
Sundance Channel
Sunshine Network
TBS Superstation
TechTV
TNT
Toon Disney
Travel Channel
Trinity Broadcasting Network
TRIO
True Stories
Turner Classic Movies
Turner South
TV Land
Univision
USA Network
VH1
VH1 Classic
WAM!
WE: Women's Entertainment
The Weather Channel
Westerns
WGN Superstation
Word Network
WorldLink TV

Notes

1. Speech to British America Inc, 24 May 2001.
2. Presentation to Multi Channel News International Summit, Chicago, 10 June 2001.
3. Other conditional access systems are not so robust leading to high rates of 'channel theft', a new crime which involves unauthorised viewing of subscription channels.
4. In 1995.
5. Michael Powell, Chairman, US Federal Communications Commission, speech to British America Inc, 24 May 2001.
6. Porter's five forces.
7. This is the case on some systems where a subscriber only subscribes to free to air channels.
8. Sumner Redstone, presentation to Multichannel News International Summit, Chicago, 10 June 2001.
9. Ibid.
10. The exception was the BBC; which actually became *richer* through exorbitantly priced colour licences. The BBC is supported by a universally levied television tax (or 'licence').
11. A phrase coined by Roy Thomson, the Canadian entrepreneur who managed to secure the commercial television franchise in Scotland in the 1950s in the era of monopoly. Unfortunately for Thomson, neither the public nor the UK Treasury ever forgot his phrase.
12. Now Associate Editor of *The Economist*.
13. Quoted in the *Daily Telegraph*, 1 January 2002.
14. Quoted in the *Sunday Times*, 17 June 2001, Business Section, p.5.
15. *Business Week*, 'For telecom suppliers it's when, not if', 8 February 2002.
16. But Spanish-owned (by Telefonica).
17. With the collapse of ITV Digital, BSkyB increased its subscribers to 7.1 million anyway.
18. That the set top box be plugged into a telephone line so that it could receive interactive content and order pay per view.
19. *New Media Markets*, Volume 20, Number 16, 3 May 2002, p. 6.
20. 3 May 2002 estimates.
21. *Daily Telegraph*, 11 May 2002, p.25.
22. *Wall St Journal*, 'Most US TV Stations aren't ready for Digital', 30 April 2002.
23. See Chapter 4.
24. *Financial Times*, 26 November 2001, p.13.
25. *New Media Markets*, Volume 20, Number 2, 18 January 2002.

26. The reverse of what multi-brand consumer industries like Unilever are doing – as they get rid of 80% of their brand portfolio.

27. *Financial Times*, 23 January 2002.

28. The US, the UK and Germany, and France had different standards in terms of the number of lines used to create a television picture. They still do – although this is now eroding with the use of 'Scart' interconnection.

29. *New Media Markets*, Volume 20, Number 14, 19 April 2002, p.12.

30. For example, Kingston Communications' system in Hull.

31. *Wall Street Journal*, 'Most US Stations Aren't Ready for Deadline on Digital Upgrades', 30 April 2002.

32. *Broadband Media*, Volume 2, Number 20, 5 November 2001, p.8.

33. *Broadband Media*, Volume 2, Number 20, 5 November 2001, p.9.

34. *New Media Markets*, Volume 20, Number 16, 3 May 2002, p.8.

35. *The Sunday Times*, Business Section, 31 March 2002, p.5.

36. *BusinessWeek*, 1 April 2002, p.21.

37. Sky Subscriber Services Ltd.

38. *New Media Markets*, Volume 19, Number 40, 9 November 2001, p.4.

39. *Business Week*, 1 April 2002, p.20.

40. *Wall Street Journal*, 'PCs v. TVs', 16 April 2002.

41. News analysis, GartnerG2, 7 May 2002, Laura Behrens and Gale Daikoku.

42. *FT Creative Business*, 'How to Run a Hit Factory', 6 November 2001.

43. *Wall Street Journal*, 'PCs v. TV', Anthony Perkins, 16 April 2002.

44. *Financial Times*, 'Creative Media', 16 April 2002, p.12.

45. *Wall Street Journal*, 'Digital Cable Channels Have Trouble Finding A Footing', Sally Beatty, 24 April 2002.

46. *Wall Street Journal*, 'Entrepreneur Aims to Sell Total TV', Rebecca Buckman, 16 April 2002.

47. *Wall Street Journal*, 'Fox's fall season to include time changes', Joe Flint, 17 May 2002.

48. Director of Television at the BBC, then CEO Channel 4, now CEO US Entertainment Networks.

49. See *No Logo*, Naomi Klein.

50. Bell Pottinger Online Strategy, 4 April 2002.

51. By *Campaign* magazine.

52. *New Media Markets*, 18 January 2002 p.6.

53. *Business Week*, 21 January 2002.

54. *Financial Times*, 7 December 2001.

55. As on 18 March 2002.

56. *Business Week*, 'MTV's World', 18 February 2002.

57. *New Media Markets*, 25 January 2002, p.3.

58. *New Media Markets*, February 2002, p.7.

59. *Daily Telegraph*, 'BBC Forces Viewers to Record', 30 May 2002, p.1.

Index